REMEMBERIN(

ESSAYS & POETRY
IN DEDICATION TO
THE ROMANTIC POET

By

VARIOUS

Read & Co.

Copyright © 2021 Ragged Hand

This edition is published by Ragged Hand,
an imprint of Read & Co.

This book is copyright and may not be reproduced or copied in any
way without the express permission of the publisher in writing.

British Library Cataloguing-in-Publication Data
A catalogue record for this book is available
from the British Library.

Read & Co. is part of Read Books Ltd.
For more information visit
www.readandcobooks.co.uk

CONTENTS

John Keats

An English poet, born in London in 1795 or 1796, died in Rome, Feb. 27, 1821. He was sent at an early age with his two brothers to a school in Enfield, where he remained until his 15th year. He seems to have been careless of the ordinary school distinctions, but read whatever authors attracted his fancy. He never advanced in his classical studies beyond Latin, and his knowledge of Greek mythology was derived from Lempriere's dictionary and Tooke's *Pantheon*; a singular fact considering the thoroughly Hellenic spirit which imbues some of his works. In 1810 he was removed from school, and apprenticed for five years to a surgeon in Edmonton. His earliest known verses are the lines *In Imitation of Spenser*.

About the same time he became acquainted with Homer through Chapman's translation, and commemorated his emotions in the sonnet, *On first looking into Chapman's Homer*. Upon the completion of his apprenticeship he removed to London to "walk the hospitals," and made the acquaintance of Leigh Hunt, Haydon, Hazlitt, Godwin, and other literary men, incited by whose praise he published a volume of poems, comprising sonnets, poetical epistles, and other small pieces, which excited little attention. He soon perceived that the profession of a surgeon was unfitted for him, both on account of his extreme nervousness in the performance of operations, and of the state of his health; and in the spring of 1817 he was induced by symptoms of consumption to make a visit to the country.

During this absence he commenced his *Endymion*, which, with some miscellaneous pieces, was published in the following year.

Keats had allied himself with a political and literary coterie obnoxious to the *Quarterly Review* and *Blackwood's Magazine*, and the appearance of a volume of poems by a new writer of the "cockney school" was the signal for an attack upon him by these periodicals, the bitterness of which savored more of personal animosity than of critical discernment. The insulting allusions to his private affairs and his family aroused in the poet no other feeling than contempt or indignation; and if we may judge from his letters, far from being crushed in spirit by the virulence of his reviewers, he would have been much more inclined to inflict personal chastisement upon them if he had met them.

Byron in *Don Juan*, and Shelley in *Adonais*, have apparently confirmed the notion that his sensitive nature on this occasion received a shock from which it never recovered; but the effect of the criticism has been greatly exaggerated. His health was failing rapidly, but from other causes. His younger brother's death in the autumn of 1818 affected him deeply, and about the same time he experienced a passion for a lady of remarkable beauty, the effect of which upon a frame worn by disease was fatal. His little patrimony became exhausted, and he began to think of making literature his profession. While preparing a third volume for the press he was attacked with a violent spitting of blood. After a long illness he recovered sufficiently to think of resuming his literary avocations, but found his mind too unstrung by sickness and the passion which had such an influence over him. In this emergency he had nearly determined to accept the berth of surgeon in an Indiaman, when a return of the previous alarming symptoms made it apparent that nothing but a winter in a milder climate would offer a chance of saving his life.

Before his departure he published a volume containing his odes on the *Nightingale* and the *Grecian Urn*, the poems of *Lamia*, *The Eve of St. Agnes*, *Isabella*, &c., and the magnificent fragment of *Hyperion*.

In September, 1820, Keats left England with Mr. Severn, a young artist and a devoted friend, who never left his bedside. He lingered a few months at Naples and Rome, and died at the latter place after much suffering. A few days before his death he said that he "felt the daisies growing over him." He was buried in the Protestant cemetery in Rome, near the spot where Shelley's ashes were afterward interred; and upon his tomb was inscribed the epitaph, dictated by himself:

"Here lies one whose name was writ in water."

His modest hope that "after his death he would be among the poets of England," has been more fully realized than he could have anticipated; and his influence can be traced in the poetic development of many later writers.

A BIOGRAPHY FROM
The American Cyclopædia, Edition of 1879

ESSAYS

KEATS

By James Russell Lowell

There are few poets whose works contain slighter hints of their personal history than those of Keats; yet there are, perhaps, even fewer whose real lives, or rather the conditions upon which they lived, are more clearly traceable in what they have written. To write the life of a man was formerly understood to mean the cataloguing and placing of circumstances, of those things which stood about the life and were more or less related to it, but were not the life itself. But Biography from day to day holds dates cheaper and facts dearer. A man's life, so far as its outward events are concerned, may be made for him, as his clothes are by the tailor, of this cut or that, of finer or coarser material; but the gait and gesture show through, and give to trappings, in themselves characterless, an individuality that belongs to the man himself. It is those essential facts which underlie the life and make the individual man that are of importance, and it is the cropping out of these upon the surface that gives us indications by which to judge of the true nature hidden below. Every man has his block given him, and the figure he cuts will depend very much upon the shape of that,—upon the knots and twists which existed in it from the beginning. We were designed in the cradle, perhaps earlier, and it is in finding out this design, and shaping ourselves to it, that our years are spent wisely. It is the vain endeavor to make ourselves what we are not that has strewn history with so many broken purposes and lives left in the rough.

Keats hardly lived long enough to develop a well-outlined character, for that results commonly from the resistance made by temperament to the many influences by which the world, as it may happen then to be, endeavors to mould every one in its own image. What his temperament was we can see clearly, and also that it subordinated itself more and more to the discipline of art.

* * * * *

John Keats, the second of four children, like Chaucer and Spenser, was a Londoner, but, unlike them, he was certainly not of gentle blood. Lord Houghton, who seems to have had a kindly wish to create him gentleman by brevet, says that he was "born in the upper ranks of the middle class." This shows a commendable tenderness for the nerves of English society, and reminds one of Northcote's story of the violin-player who, wishing to compliment his pupil, George III., divided all fiddlers into three classes,—those who could not play at all, those who played very badly, and those who played very well,—assuring his Majesty that he had made such commendable progress as to have already reached the second rank. We shall not be too greatly shocked by knowing that the father of Keats (as Lord Houghton had told us in an earlier biography) "was employed in the establishment of Mr. Jennings, the proprietor of large livery-stables on the Pavement in Moorfields, nearly opposite the entrance into Finsbury Circus." So that, after all, it was not so bad; for, first, Mr. Jennings was a proprietor; second, he was the proprietor of an establishment; third, he was the proprietor of a large establishment; and fourth, this large establishment was nearly opposite Finsbury Circus,—a name which vaguely dilates the imagination with all sorts of potential grandeurs. It is true Leigh Hunt asserts that Keats "was a little too sensitive on the score of his origin," but we can find no trace of such a feeling either in his poetry or in such of his letters as have been printed. We suspect the fact to have been that he resented with becoming pride the vulgar Blackwood and Quarterly standard, which measured genius by genealogies. It is enough that his poetical pedigree is of the best, tracing through Spenser to Chaucer, and that Pegasus does not stand at livery even in the largest establishments in Moorfields.

As well as we can make out, then, the father of Keats was a groom in the service of Mr. Jennings, and married the daughter of his master. Thus, on the mother's side, at least, we find a grandfather, on the father's there is no hint of such an ancestor, and we must charitably take him for granted. It is of more importance that the elder Keats was a man of sense and energy, and that his wife was a "lively and intelligent woman, who hastened the birth of the poet by her passionate love of amusement," bringing him into the world, a seven-months' child, on the 29th October, 1795, instead of the 29th of December, as would have been conventionally proper. Lord Houghton describes her as "tall, with a large oval face, and a somewhat saturnine demeanour." This last circumstance does not agree very well with what he had just before told us of her liveliness, but he consoles us by adding that "she succeeded, however, in inspiring her children with the profoundest affection." This was particularly true of John, who once, when between four and five years old, mounted guard at her chamber door with an old sword, when she was ill and the doctor had ordered her not to be disturbed.

In 1804, Keats being in his ninth year, his father was killed by a fall from his horse. His mother seems to have been ambitious for her children, and there was some talk of sending John to Harrow. Fortunately this plan was thought too expensive, and he was sent instead to the school of Mr. Clarke at Enfield with his brothers. A maternal uncle, who had distinguished himself by his courage under Duncan at Camperdown, was the hero of his nephews, and they went to school resolved to maintain the family reputation for courage. John was always fighting, and was chiefly noted among his school-fellows as a strange compound of pluck and sensibility. He attacked an usher who had boxed his brother's ears; and when his mother died, in 1810, was moodily inconsolable, hiding himself for several days in a nook under the master's desk, and refusing all comfort from teacher or friend.

He was popular at school, as boys of spirit always are, and impressed his companions with a sense of his power. They thought he would one day be a famous soldier. This may have been owing to the stories he told them of the heroic uncle, whose deeds, we may be sure, were properly famoused by the boy Homer, and whom they probably took for an admiral at the least, as it would have been well for Keats's literary prosperity if he had been. At any rate, they thought John would be a great man, which is the main thing, for the public opinion of the playground is truer and more discerning than that of the world, and if you tell us what the boy was, we will tell you what the man longs to be, however he may be repressed by necessity or fear of the police reports.

Lord Houghton has failed to discover anything else especially worthy of record in the school-life of Keats. He translated the twelve books of the Aeneid, read Robinson Crusoe and the Incas of Peru, and looked into Shakespeare. He left school in 1810, with little Latin and no Greek, but he had studied Spence's Polymetis, Tooke's Pantheon, and Lempriere's Dictionary, and knew gods, nymphs, and heroes, which were quite as good company perhaps for him as artists and aspirates. It is pleasant to fancy the horror of those respectable writers if their pages could suddenly have become alive tinder their pens with all that the young poet saw in them.

On leaving school he was apprenticed for five years to a surgeon at Edmonton. His master was a Mr. Hammond, "of some eminence" in his profession, as Lord Houghton takes care to assure us. The place was of more importance than the master, for its neighborhood to Enfield enabled him to keep up his intimacy with the family of his former teacher, Mr. Clarke, and to borrow books of them. In 1812, when he was in his seventeenth year, Mr. Charles Cowden Clarke lent him the "Faerie Queene." Nothing that is told of Orpheus or Amphion is more wonderful than this miracle of Spenser's, transforming a surgeon's apprentice into a great poet. Keats learned at once the secret of his birth, and henceforward his indentures ran to Apollo instead of Mr. Hammond. Thus could the Muse defend her son. It is the old story,—the lost heir discovered by his aptitude for what is gentle and knightly. Haydon tells us "that he used sometimes to say to his brother he feared he should never be a poet, and if he was not he would destroy himself." This was perhaps a half-conscious reminiscence of Chatterton, with whose genius and fate he had an intense sympathy, it may be from an inward foreboding of the shortness of his own career.

Before long we find him studying Chaucer, then Shakespeare, and afterward Milton. But Chapman's translations had a more abiding influence on his style both for good and evil. That he read wisely, his comments on the "Paradise Lost" are enough to prove. He now also commenced poet himself, but does not appear to have neglected the study of his profession. He was a youth of energy and purpose, and though he no doubt penned many a stanza when he should have been anatomizing, and walked the hospitals accompanied by the early gods, nevertheless passed a very creditable examination in 1817. In the spring of this year, also, he prepared to take his first degree as poet, and accordingly published a small volume containing a selection of his earlier essays in verse. It attracted little attention, and the rest of this year seems to have been occupied with a journey on foot in Scotland, and the composition of "Endymion," which was published in 1818. Milton's "Tetrachordon" was not better abused; but Milton's assailants were unorganized, and were obliged each to print and pay for his own dingy little quarto, trusting to the natural laws of demand and supply to furnish him with readers. Keats was arraigned by the constituted authorities of literary justice. They might be, nay, they were Jeffrieses and Scroggses, but the sentence was published, and the penalty inflicted before all England. The difference between his fortune and Milton's was that between being pelted by a mob of personal enemies and being set in the pillory. In the first case, the annoyance brushes off mostly with the mud; in the last, there is no solace but the consciousness of suffering in a great cause. This solace, to a certain extent, Keats had; for his ambition was noble, and he hoped not to make a great reputation, but to be a great poet. Haydon says that Wordsworth and Keats were the only men he had ever seen who looked conscious of a lofty purpose.

It is curious that men should resent more fiercely what they suspect to be good verses, than what they know to be bad morals. Is it because they feel themselves incapable of the one and not of the other? Probably a certain amount of honest loyalty to old idols in danger of dethronement is to be taken into account, and quite as much of the cruelty of criticism is due to want of thought as to deliberate injustice. However it be, the best poetry has been the most savagely attacked, and men who scrupulously practised the Ten Commandments as if there were never a not in any of them, felt every sentiment of their better nature outraged by the "Lyrical Ballads." It is idle to attempt to show that Keats did not suffer keenly from the vulgarities of Blackwood and the Quarterly. He suffered in proportion as his ideal was high, and he was conscious of falling below it. In England, especially, it is not pleasant to be ridiculous, even if you are a lord; but to be ridiculous and an apothecary at the same time is almost as bad as it was formerly to be excommunicated. A priori, there was something absurd in poetry written by the son of an assistant in the livery-stables of Mr. Jennings, even though they were an establishment, and a large establishment, and nearly opposite Finsbury Circus. Mr. Gifford, the ex-cobbler, thought so in the Quarterly, and Mr. Terry, the actor, thought so even more distinctly in Blackwood, bidding the young apothecary "back to his gallipots!" It is not pleasant to be talked down upon by your inferiors who happen to have the advantage of position, nor to be drenched with ditchwater, though you know it to be thrown by a scullion in a garret.

Keats, as his was a temperament in which sensibility was

excessive, could not but be galled by this treatment. He was galled the more that he was also a man of strong sense, and capable of understanding clearly how hard it is to make men acknowledge solid value in a person whom they have once heartily laughed at. Reputation is in itself only a farthing-candle, of wavering and uncertain flame, and easily blown out, but it is the light by which the world looks for and finds merit. Keats longed for fame, but longed above all to deserve it. To his friend Taylor he writes, "There is but one way for me. The road lies through study, application, and thought." Thrilling with the electric touch of sacred leaves, he saw in vision, like Dante, that small procession of the elder poets to which only elect centuries can add another laurelled head. Might he, too, deserve from posterity the love and reverence which he paid to those antique glories? It was no unworthy ambition, but everything was against him,—birth, health, even friends, since it was partly on their account that he was sneered at. His very name stood in his way, for Fame loves best such, syllables as are sweet and sonorous on the tongue, like Spenserian, Shakespearian. In spite of Juliet, there is a great deal in names, and when the fairies come with their gifts to the cradle of the selected child, let one, wiser than the rest, choose a name for him from which well-sounding derivatives can be made, and, best of all, with a termination in on. Men judge the current coin of opinion by the ring, and are readier to take without question whatever is Platonic, Baconian, Newtonian, Johnsonian, Washingtonian, Jeffersonian, Napoleonic, and all the rest. You cannot make a good adjective out of Keats,—the more pity,—and to say a thing is Keatsy is to contemn it. Fortune likes fine names.

Haydon tells us that Keats was very much depressed by the fortunes of his book. This was natural enough, but he took it all in a manly way, and determined to revenge himself by writing better poetry. He knew that activity, and not despondency, is the true counterpoise to misfortune. Haydon is sure of the change in his spirits, because he would come to the painting-room and sit silent for hours. But we rather think that the conversation, where Mr. Haydon was, resembled that in a young author's first play, where the other interlocutors are only brought in as convenient points for the hero to hitch the interminable web of his monologue upon. Besides, Keats had been continuing his education this year, by a course of Elgin marbles and pictures by the great Italians, and might very naturally have found little to say about Mr. Haydon's extensive works, that he would have cared to hear. Lord Houghton, on the other hand, in his eagerness to prove that Keats was not killed by the article in the Quarterly, is carried too far toward the opposite extreme, and more than hints that he was not even hurt by it. This would have been true of Wordsworth, who, by a constant companionship with mountains, had acquired something of their manners, but was simply impossible to a man of Keats's temperament.

On the whole, perhaps, we need not respect Keats the less for having been gifted with sensibility, and may even say what we believe to be true, that his health was injured by the failure of his book. A man cannot have a sensuous nature and be pachydermatous at the same time, and if he be imaginative as well as sensuous, he suffers just in proportion to the amount of his imagination. It is perfectly true that what we call the world, in these affairs, is nothing more than a mere Brocken spectre, the projected shadow of ourselves; but as long as we do not know it, it is a very passable giant. We are not without experience of natures so purely intellectual that their bodies had no more concern in their mental doings and sufferings than a house has with the good or ill fortune of its occupant. But poets are not built on this plan, and especially poets like Keats, in whom the moral seems to have so perfectly interfused the physical man, that you might almost say he could feel sorrow with his hands, so truly did his body, like that of Donne's Mistress Boulstred, think and remember and forebode. The healthiest poet of whom our civilization has been capable says that when he beholds

"desert a beggar born,
And strength by limping sway disabled,
And art made tongue-tied by authority,"

alluding, plainly enough, to the Giffords of his day,

"And simple truth miscalled simplicity,"

as it was long afterward in Wordsworth's case,

"And captive Good attending Captain Ill,"

that then even he, the poet to whom, of all others, life seems to have been dearest, as it was also the fullest of enjoyment, "tired of all these," had nothing for it but to cry for "restful Death."

Keats, to all appearance, accepted his ill fortune courageously. He certainly did not overestimate "Endymion," and perhaps a sense of humor which was not wanting in him may have served as a buffer against the too importunate shock of disappointment. "He made Ritchie promise," says Haydon, "he would carry his 'Endymion' to the great desert of Sahara and fling it in the midst." On the 9th October, 1818, he writes to his publisher, Mr. Hessey, "I cannot but feel indebted to those gentlemen who have taken my part. As for the rest, I begin to get acquainted with my own strength and weakness. Praise or blame has but a momentary effect on the man whose love of beauty in the abstract makes him a severe critic of his own works. My own domestic criticism has given me pain without comparison beyond what Blackwood or the Quarterly could inflict; and also, when I feel I am right, no external praise can give me such a glow as my own solitary reperception and ratification of what is fine. J.S. is perfectly right in regard to 'the slipshod Endymion.' That it is so is no fault of mine. No! though it may sound a little paradoxical, it is as good as I had power to make it by myself. Had I been nervous about its being a perfect piece, and with that view asked advice and trembled over every page, it would not have been written; for it is not in my nature to fumble. I will write independently. I have written independently without judgment. I may write independently and with judgment, hereafter. The Genius of Poetry must work out its own salvation in a man. It cannot be matured by law and precept, but by sensation and watchfulness in itself. That which is creative must create itself. In 'Endymion' I leaped headlong into the sea, and thereby have become better acquainted with the soundings, the quicksands, and the rocks, than if I had stayed upon the green shore, and piped a silly pipe, and took tea and comfortable advice. I was never afraid of failure; for I would sooner fail than not be among the greatest."

This was undoubtedly true, and it was naturally the side which a large-minded person would display to a friend. This is what he thought, but whether it was what he felt, I think doubtful. I look upon it rather as one of the phenomena of that multanimous nature of the poet, which makes him for the moment that of which he has an intellectual perception. Elsewhere he says something which seems to hint at the true state of the case. "I must think that difficulties nerve the spirit of a man: they make our prime objects a refuge as well as a passion." One cannot help contrasting Keats with Wordsworth,—the one altogether poet; the other essentially a Wordsworth, with the poetic faculty added,—the one shifting from form to form, and from style to style, and pouring his hot throbbing life into every mould; the other remaining always the individual, producing works, and not so much living in his poems as memorially recording his life in them. When Wordsworth alludes to the foolish criticisms on his writings, he speaks serenely and generously of Wordsworth the poet, as if he were an unbiassed third person, who takes up the argument merely in the interest of literature. He towers into a bald egotism which is quite above and beyond selfishness. Poesy was his employment; it was Keats's very existence, and he felt the rough treatment of his verses as if it had been the wounding of a limb. To Wordsworth, composing was a healthy exercise, his slow pulse and imperturbable self trust gave him assurance of a life so long that he could wait, and when we read his poems we should never suspect the existence in him of any sense but that of observation, as if Wordsworth the poet were a half-mad land-surveyor, accompanied by Mr. Wordsworth the distributor of stamps, as a kind of keeper. But every one of Keats's poems was a sacrifice of vitality, a virtue went away from him into every one of them; even yet, as we turn the leaves, they seem to warm and thrill our fingers with the flush of his fine senses, and the flutter of his electrical nerves, and we do not wonder he felt that what he did was to be done swiftly.

In the mean time his younger brother languished and died, his elder seems to have been in some way unfortunate and had gone to America, and Keats himself showed symptoms of the hereditary disease which caused his death at last. It is in October, 1818, that we find the first allusion to a passion which was, erelong, to consume him It is plain enough beforehand, that those were not moral or mental graces that should attract a man like Keats. His intellect was satisfied and absorbed by his art, his books, and his friends He could have companionship and appreciation from men; what he craved of woman was only repose. That luxurious nature, which would have tossed uneasily on a crumpled rose leaf, must have something softer to rest upon than intellect, something less ethereal than culture. It was his body that needed to have its equilibrium restored, the waste of his nervous energy that must be repaired by deep draughts of the overflowing life and drowsy tropical force of an abundant and healthily poised womanhood. Writing to his sister-in-law, he says of this nameless person: "She is not a Cleopatra, but is, at least, a Charmian; she has a rich Eastern look; she has fine eyes and fine manners. When she comes into a room she makes the same impression as the beauty of a leopardess. She is too fine and too conscious of herself to repulse any man who may address her. From habit, she thinks that nothing particular. I always find myself at ease with such a woman; the picture before me always gives me a life and animation which I cannot possibly feel with anything inferior. I am at such times too much occupied in admiring to be awkward or in a tremble. I forget myself entirely, because I live in her. You will by this time think I am in love with her, so, before I go any farther, I will tell you that I am not. She kept me awake one night, as a tune of Mozart's might do. I speak of the thing as a pastime and an amusement, than which I can feel none deeper than a conversation with an imperial woman, the very yes and no of whose life is to me a banquet . . . I like her and her like, because one has no sensation; what we both are is taken for granted . . . She walks across a room in such a manner that a man is drawn toward her with magnetic power . . . I believe, though, she has faults, the same as a Cleopatra or a Charmian might have had. Yet she is a fine thing, speaking in a worldly way; for there are two distinct tempers of mind in which we judge of things,—the worldly, theatrical, and pantomimical; and the unearthly, spiritual, and ethereal. In the former, Bonaparte, Lord Byron, and this Charmian hold the first place in our minds; in the latter, John Howard, Bishop Hooker rocking his child's cradle, and you, my dear sister, are the conquering feelings. As a man of the world, I love the rich talk of a Charmian; as an eternal being, I love the thought of you. I should like her to ruin me, and I should like you to save me."

It is pleasant always to see Love hiding his head with such pains, while his whole body is so clearly visible, as in this extract. This lady, it seems, is not a Cleopatra, only a Charmian; but presently we find that she is imperial. He does not love her, but he would just like to be ruined by her, nothing more. This glimpse of her, with her leopardess beauty, crossing the room and drawing men after her magnetically, is all we have. She seems to have been still living in 1848, and as Lord Houghton tells us, kept the memory of the poet sacred. "She is an East-Indian," Keats says, "and ought to be her grandfather's heir." Her name we do not know. It appears from Dilke's "Papers of a Critic" that they were betrothed: "It is quite a settled thing between John Keats and Miss ——. God help them. It is a bad thing for them. The mother says she cannot prevent it, and that her only hope is that it will go off. He don't like any one to look at her or to speak to her." Alas, the tropical warmth became a consuming fire!

"His passion cruel grown took on a hue
Fierce and sanguineous."

Between this time and the spring of 1820 he seems to have worked assiduously. Of course, worldly success was of more importance than ever. He began "Hyperion," but had given it up in September, 1819, because, as he said, "there were too many Miltonic inversions in it." He wrote "Lamia" after an attentive study of Dryden's versification. This period also produced the "Eve of St. Agnes," "Isabella," and the odes to the "Nightingale" and to the "Grecian Urn." He studied Italian, read Ariosto, and wrote part of a humorous poem, "The Cap and Bells." He tried his hand at tragedy, and Lord Houghton has published among his "Remains," "Otho the Great," and all that was ever written of "King Stephen." We think he did unwisely, for a biographer is hardly called upon to show how ill his biographee could do anything.

In the winter of 1820 he was chilled in riding on the top of a stage-coach, and came home in a state of feverish excitement. He was persuaded to go to bed, and in getting between the cold sheets, coughed slightly. "That is blood in my mouth," he said; "bring me the candle; let me see this blood." It was of a brilliant red, and his medical knowledge enabled him to interpret the augury. Those narcotic odors that seem to breathe seaward, and steep in repose the senses of the voyager who is drifting toward the shore of the mysterious Other World, appeared to envelop him, and, looking up with sudden calmness, he said, "I know the color of that blood; it is arterial blood; I cannot be deceived in that color. That drop is my death-warrant; I must die."

There was a slight rally during the summer of that year, but toward autumn he grew worse again, and it was decided that he should go to Italy. He was accompanied thither by his friend, Mr. Severn, an artist. After embarking, he wrote to his friend, Mr. Brown. We give a part of this letter, which is so deeply tragic that the sentences we take almost seem to break away from the rest with a cry of anguish, like the branches of Dante's lamentable wood.

"I wish to write on subjects that will not agitate me much. There is one I must mention and have done with it. Even if my body would recover of itself, this would prevent it. The very thing which I want to live most for will be a great occasion of my death. I cannot help it. Who can help it? Were I in health it would make me ill, and how can I bear it in my state? I dare say you will be able to guess on what subject I am harping,—you know what was my greatest pain during the first part of my illness at your house I wish for death every day and night to deliver me from these pains, and then I wish death away, for death would destroy even those pains, which are better than nothing. Land and sea, weakness and decline, are great separators, but Death is the great divorcer forever. When the pang of this thought has passed through my mind, I may say the bitterness of death is passed. I often wish for you, that you might flatter me with the best. I think, without my mentioning it, for my sake, you would be a, friend to Miss —— when I am dead. You think she has many faults, but for my sake think she has not one. If there is anything you can do for her by word or deed I know you will do it. I am in a state at present in which woman, merely as woman, can have no more power over me than stocks and stones, and yet the difference of my sensations with respect to Miss —— and my sister is amazing,—the one seems to absorb the other to a degree incredible. I seldom think of my brother and sister in America; the thought of leaving Miss —— is beyond everything horrible,—the sense of darkness coming over me,—I eternally

24

see her figure eternally vanishing, some of the phrases she was in the habit of using during my last nursing at Wentworth Place ring in my ears. Is there another life? Shall I awake and find all this a dream? There must be; we cannot be created for this sort of suffering."

To the same friend he writes again from Naples, 1st November, 1820:—

"The persuasion that I shall see her no more will kill me. My dear Brown, I should have had her when I was in health, and I should have remained well. I can bear to die,—I cannot bear to leave her. O God! God! God! Everything I have in my trunks that reminds me of her goes through me like a spear. The silk lining she put in my travelling-cap scalds my head. My imagination is horribly vivid about her,—I see her, I hear her. There is nothing in the world of sufficient interest to divert me from her a moment. This was the case when I was in England, I cannot recollect, without shuddering, the time that I was a prisoner at Hunt's, and used to keep my eyes fixed on Hampstead all day. Then there was a good hope of seeing her again,—now!—O that I could be buried near where she lives! I am afraid to write to her, to receive a letter from her,—to see her handwriting would break my heart. Even to hear of her anyhow, to see her name written, would be more than I can bear. My dear Brown, what am I to do? Where can I look for consolation or ease? If I had any chance of recovery, this passion would kill me. Indeed, through the whole of my illness, both at your house and at Kentish Town, this fever has never ceased wearing me out."

The two friends went almost immediately from Naples to Rome, where Keats was treated with great kindness by the distinguished physician, Dr. (afterward Sir James) Clark. But there was no hope from the first. His disease was beyond remedy, as his heart was beyond comfort. The very fact that life might be happy deepened his despair. He might not have sunk so soon, but the waves in which he was struggling looked only the blacker that they were shone upon by the signal-torch that promised safety and love and rest.

It is good to know that one of Keats's last pleasures was in hearing Severn read aloud from a volume of Jeremy Taylor. On first coming to Rome, he had bought a copy of Alfieri, but, finding on the second page these lines,

> "Misera me! sollievo a me non resta
> Altro che il pianto, ed il pianto é delitto,"

he laid down the book and opened it no more. On the 14th February, 1821, Severn speaks of a change that had taken place in him toward greater quietness and peace. He talked much, and fell at last into a sweet sleep, in which he seemed to have happy dreams. Perhaps he heard the soft footfall of the angel of Death, pacing to and fro under his window, to be his Valentine. That night he asked to have this epitaph inscribed upon his gravestone,—

> "HERE LIES ONE WHOSE NAME WAS WRIT IN WATER."

On the 23d he died, without pain and as if falling asleep. His last words were, "I am dying; I shall die easy; don't be frightened, be firm and thank God it has come!"

He was buried in the Protestant burial-ground at Rome, in that part of it which is now disused and secluded from the rest. A short time before his death he told Severn that he thought his intensest pleasure in life had been to watch the growth of flowers; and once, after lying peacefully awhile, he said, "I feel the flowers growing over me." His grave is marked by a little headstone on which are carved somewhat rudely his name and age, and the epitaph dictated by himself. No tree or shrub has been planted near it, but the daisies, faithful to their buried lover, crowd his small mound with a galaxy of their innocent stars, more prosperous than those under which he lived. In person, Keats was below the middle height, with a head small in proportion to the breadth of his shoulders. His hair was brown and fine, falling in natural ringlets about a face in which energy and sensibility were remarkably mixed. Every feature was delicately cut; the chin was bold; and about the mouth something of a pugnacious expression. His eyes were mellow and glowing, large, dark, and sensitive. At the recital of a noble action or a beautiful thought they would suffuse with tears, and his mouth trembled. Haydon says that his eyes had an inward Delphian look that was perfectly divine.

The faults of Keats's poetry are obvious enough, but it should be remembered that he died at twenty-five, and that he offends by superabundance and not poverty. That he was overlanguaged at first there can be no doubt, and in this was implied the possibility of falling back to the perfect mean of diction. It is only by the rich that the costly plainness, which at once satisfies the taste and the imagination, is attainable.

Whether Keats was original or not, I do not think it useful to discuss until it has been settled what originality is. Lord Houghton tells us that this merit (whatever it is) has been denied to Keats, because his poems take the color of the authors he happened to be reading at the time he wrote them. But men have their intellectual ancestry, and the likeness of some one of them is forever unexpectedly flashing out in the features of a descendant, it may be after a gap of several generations. In the parliament of the present every man represents a constituency of the past. It is true that Keats has the accent of the men from whom he learned to speak, but this is to make originality a mere question of externals, and in this sense the author of a dictionary might bring an action of trover against every author who used his words. It is the man behind the words that gives them value, and if Shakespeare help himself to a verse or a phrase, it is with ears that have learned of him to listen that we feel the harmony of the one, and it is the mass of his intellect that makes the other weighty with meaning. Enough that we recognize in Keats that indefinable newness and unexpectedness which we call genius.

27

The sunset is original every evening, though for thousands of years it has built out of the same light and vapor its visionary cities with domes and pinnacles, and its delectable mountains which night shall utterly abase and destroy.

Three men, almost contemporaneous with each other,—Wordsworth, Keats, and Byron,—were the great means of bringing back English poetry from the sandy deserts of rhetoric, and recovering for her her triple inheritance of simplicity, sensuousness, and passion. Of these, Wordsworth was the only conscious reformer, and his hostility to the existing formalism injured his earlier poems by tingeing them with something of iconoclastic extravagance. He was the deepest thinker, Keats the most essentially a poet, and Byron the most keenly intellectual of the three. Keats had the broadest mind, or at least his mind was open on more sides, and he was able to understand Wordsworth and judge Byron, equally conscious, through his artistic sense, of the greatnesses of the one and the many littlenesses of the other, while Wordsworth was isolated in a feeling of his prophetic character, and Byron had only an uneasy and jealous instinct of contemporary merit. The poems of Wordsworth, as he was the most individual, accordingly reflect the moods of his own nature; those of Keats, from sensitiveness of organization, the moods of his own taste and feeling; and those of Byron, who was impressible chiefly through the understanding, the intellectual and moral wants of the time in which he lived. Wordsworth has influenced most the ideas of succeeding poets; Keats, their forms; and Byron, interesting to men of imagination less for his writings than for what his writings indicate, reappears no more in poetry, but presents an ideal to youth made restless with vague desires not yet regulated by experience nor supplied with motives by the duties of life.

Keats certainly had more of the penetrative and sympathetic imagination which belongs to the poet, of that imagination which identifies itself with the momentary object of its contemplation, than any man of these later days. It is not merely that he has studied the Elizabethans and caught their turn of thought, but that he really sees things with their sovereign eye, and feels them with their electrified senses. His imagination was his bliss and bane. Was he cheerful, he "hops about the gravel with the sparrows"; was he morbid, he "would reject a Petrarcal coronation,—on account of my dying day, and because women have cancers." So impressible was he as to say that he "had no nature," meaning character. But he knew what the faculty was worth, and says finely, "The imagination may be compared to Adam's dream: he awoke and found it truth." He had an unerring instinct for the poetic uses of things, and for him they had no other use. We are apt to talk of the classic renaissance as of a phenomenon long past, nor ever to be renewed, and to think the Greeks and Romans alone had the mighty magic to work such a miracle. To me one of the most interesting aspects of Keats is that in him we have an example of the renaissance going on almost under our own eyes, and that the intellectual ferment was in him kindled by a purely English leaven. He had properly no scholarship, any more than Shakespeare had, but like him he assimilated at a touch whatever could serve his purpose. His delicate senses absorbed culture at every pore. Of the self-denial to which he trained himself (unexampled in one so young) the second draft of Hyperion as compared with the first is a conclusive proof. And far indeed is his "Lamia" from the lavish indiscrimination of "Endymion." In his Odes he showed a sense of form and proportion which we seek vainly in almost any other English poet, and some of his sonnets (taking all qualities into consideration) are the most perfect in our language. No doubt there is something tropical and of strange overgrowth in his sudden maturity, but it was maturity nevertheless. Happy the young poet who has the saving fault of exuberance, if he have also the shaping faculty that sooner or later will amend it!

As every young person goes through all the world-old experiences, fancying them something peculiar and personal to himself, so it is with every new generation, whose youth always finds its representatives in its poets. Keats rediscovered the delight and wonder that lay enchanted in the dictionary. Wordsworth revolted at the poetic diction which he found in vogue, but his own language rarely rises above it, except when it is upborne by the thought. Keats had an instinct for fine words, which are in themselves pictures and ideas, and had more of the power of poetic expression than any modern English poet. And by poetic expression I do not mean merely a vividness in particulars, but the right feeling which heightens or subdues a passage or a whole poem to the proper tone, and gives entireness to the effect. There is a great deal more than is commonly supposed in this choice of words. Men's thoughts and opinions are in a great degree vassals of him who invents a new phrase or reapplies an old epithet. The thought or feeling a thousand times repeated becomes his at last who utters it best. This power of language is veiled in the old legends which make the invisible powers the servants of some word. As soon as we have discovered the word for our joy or sorrow we are no longer its serfs, but its lords. We reward the discoverer of an anaesthetic for the body and make him member of all the societies, but him who finds a nepenthe for the soul we elect into the small academy of the immortals.

The poems of Keats mark an epoch in English poetry; for, however often we may find traces of it in others, in them found its most unconscious expression that reaction against the barrel-organ style which had been reigning by a kind of sleepy divine right for half a century. The lowest point was indicated when there was such an utter confounding of the common and the uncommon sense that Dr. Johnson wrote verse and Burke prose. The most profound gospel of criticism was, that nothing was good poetry that could not be translated into good prose, as if one should say that the test of sufficient moonlight was that tallow-candles could be made of it. We find Keats at first going to the other extreme, and endeavoring to extract green cucumbers from the rays of tallow; but we see also incontestable proof of the greatness and purity of his poetic gift in the constant return toward equilibrium and repose in his later poems. And it is a repose always lofty and clear-aired, like that of the eagle balanced in incommunicable sunshine. In him a vigorous understanding developed itself in equal measure with the divine faculty; thought emancipated itself from expression without becoming its tyrant; and music and meaning floated together, accordant as swan and shadow, on the smooth element of his verse. Without losing its sensuousness, his poetry refined itself and grew more inward, and the sensational was elevated into the typical by the control of that finer sense which underlies the senses and is the spirit of them.

ON THE
PROMISE OF KEATS

By George Edward Woodberry

In the domestic, chatty, and nonsense portions of the letters of
Keats, in their chaffing, their abandon, their unregarded laughter
(and admirable fooling they are, too), there is a spontaneous
and irresponsible gayety, which, being quite natural only to the
young heart and mind, charmingly discloses his youthfulness as
a prime quality. Of all the famous English poets, he had most of
the spirit of April in him. His senses were keen; his temperament
was feverish, now jealous and irritable, and straightway humble
and indulgent; his imaginary joys and sorrows were spiritual
possessions, subjecting him; his humor was scampering, his
fancy teeming, his taste erratic, his critical faculty exposed to
balking enthusiasms; his opinions of men and affairs were hasty,
circumscribed, frequently adopted unreflectingly at second-
hand; and, with all these boyish traits, he was extremely self-
absorbed. At the centre of his individuality, nevertheless, was
the elemental spark, the saving power of genius, the temperance,
sanity, and self-reverence of a fine nature gradually coming to
the knowledge of its faculties and unriddling the secret of its
own moral beauty. Hence Lord Houghton, doing more essential
justice to Keats than any of his louder eulogists, describes his
works as rather the exercises of his poetical education than
the charactery of his original and free power; and Matthew
Arnold, even when placing him with Shakespeare, excuses him
as a 'prentice hand in the wisest art. Too many of his admirers,
seizing upon the external, accidental, and temporal in his

33

biography and the fragmentary and parasitical in his poetry, have really wronged Keats more than did the now infamous reviews; they have rescued him from among the cockneys only to confound him with the neo-pagans. In what did the promise of Keats lie? The first step in the inquiry is the recognition of his immaturity,—the acknowledgment that his memorials must be searched for the germ rather than the fruit.

Sensuous Keats was, as every poet whose inspiration is direct from Heaven must be; unfortunately, the extraordinary beauty and facility of his descriptions of sensation, and his taste for climax and point in his prose have made it easy to quote phrases which seem to show that he was unduly attached to delights of mere sense. To pass by the anecdotes of Haydon, not too scrupulous a truth-teller, here is a characteristic paragraph written to his brother George:—

"This morning I am in a sort of temper, indolent, and supremely careless; I long after a stanza or two of Thomson's Castle of Indolence; my passions are all asleep, from my having slumbered till nearly eleven, and weakened the animal fibre all over me to a delightful sensation about three degrees this side of faintness. If I had teeth of pearl and the breath of lilies, I should call it languor; but as I am I must call it laziness. In this state of effeminacy, the fibres of the brain are relaxed in common with the rest of the body, and to such a happy degree that pleasure has no show of enticement and pain no unbearable frown; neither poetry, nor ambition, nor love have any alertness of countenance; as they pass by me, they seem rather like three figures in a Greek vase, two men and a woman, whom no one but myself could distinguish in their disguisement. This is the only happiness, and is a rare instance of advantage in the body overpowering the mind."

With similiar zest he enumerates the pleasures of drinking claret or of eating a peach, or he describes his "East Indian" to his brother's wife: "She kept me awake one night, as a tune of Mozart's might do. I speak of the thing as a pastime and an amusement, than which I can feel none deeper than a conversation with an imperial woman, the very 'yes' and 'no' of whose lips is to me a banquet . . . As a man of the world, I love the rich talk of a Charmian; as an eternal being, I love the thought of you. I should like her to ruin me, and I should like you to save me."

Such quick susceptibility to sensuous impressions of every kind may be plentifully illustrated by opening almost at random in his works. But the characteristics that mark the real sensualist—the content that the lotus-leaf vapors forth, the fierceness of the centaur's pursuit, the struggle of the faun's transformation are nowhere to be found in the letters or the poems; before his illness, at least, there is no debility, irresolution, or mastery of the instincts over the mind. In fact, without any revolution of his nature, without the slightest effort, by mere growth it would seem, he passed on into the "Chamber of Maiden Thought," as he phrased it, and became absorbed as deeply in his reflections as previously in his impulses. At no time, indeed, was he wholly unthoughtful. The passages that have been given above are parenthetical, and should be read in connection with such as these, of the opposite tenor:—

"I must think that difficulties nerve the spirit of a man; they make our prime objects a refuge as well as a passion."

"I am becoming accustomed to the privations of the pleasures of sense. In the midst of the world, I live like a hermit. I have forgot how to lay plans for the enjoyment of any pleasure. I feel I can bear anything,—any misery, even imprisonment,—so long as I have neither wife nor child."

"Women must want imagination, and they may thank God for it; and so may we, that a delicate being can feel happy without any sense of crime."

"Scenery is fine, but human nature is finer; the sward is richer for the tread of a real nervous English foot; the eagle's nest is finer for the mountaineer having looked into it."

Many a remark, based like these immediately upon his own

experience, shows that Keats had an insight into his own life and an outlook on the world inconsistent with the portrayal of him as merely impassioned with sensuous beauty.

So far, in fact, was Keats from being either lapped in Lydian airs or fed on food of sweetest melancholy that he was sometimes a disagreeably unhappy person, if his brother George's description of him be entirely true, since his moodiness was vented in complaints, irritable jealousies, and like ways. However exceptional such occasions were in the intercourse of the brothers, this exposure, taken together with some of the upbraidings in the letters to Fanny Brawne, is very significant. Keats himself refers to the strain of morbidity in him, and, although from time to time he felt the strong awakening of the philanthropic instinct, frequently expresses his distaste for society, his misanthropy, his indifference to the public, his wish to live withdrawn, free from human relations, engaged in poetizing for his own sake. Toward women especially he had a bitter tongue, before he fell in love with Fanny Brawne.

"When I was a schoolboy, I thought a fair woman a pure goddess; my mind was a soft nest in which some one of them slept, though she knew it not . . . When I am among women, I have evil thoughts, malice, spleen; I cannot speak or be silent; I am full of suspicions, and therefore listen to nothing; I am in a hurry to be gone. You must be charitable, and put all this perversity to my being disappointed since my boyhood. Yet with such feelings I am happier alone, among crowds of men, by myself, or with a friend or two."

He ascribes this peculiarity to his love for his brothers, "passing the love of women:"

"I have been ill-tempered with them, I have vexed them,—but the thought of them has always stifled the impression that any woman might otherwise have made on me."

He saw but little to choose, in his satirical moods, between men and hawks:—

"The hawk wants a mate; so does the Man. Look at them both;

36

they set about it and procure one in the same manner; they want both a nest, and they set about one in the same manner. The noble animal man, for his amusement, smokes a pipe; the hawk balances about the clouds: that is the only difference of their leisures."

Experience did not teach him more charity, though it made him more discriminating:—

"The more I know of men the more I know how to value entire liberality in any of them. Thank God, there are a great many who will sacrifice their worldly interest for a friend. I wish there were more who would sacrifice their passions. The worst of men are those whose self-interests are their passions; the next, those whose passions are their self-interest. Upon the whole, I dislike mankind. Whatever people on the other side of the question may advance, they cannot deny that they are always surprised at hearing of a good action and never of a bad one."

This temper toward man in the abstract is the general feeling of which his mood toward the public is a special instance. He simply disregarded men who stood in no intimate relation to him, whether he met them in society or wrote verses for them to read. He was not, if his word be literally taken, sensitive to criticism or ambitious of popularity: he neglected the one because he put faith in his own judgment, and he despised the other because it was to be got at a vulgar cost. His depreciation of the life of men, as he saw it, arose partly from a consciousness of power, partly from a sense of the distance between his thoughts and hopes and those of his fellows. The aloofness of genius he had in full measure. That curiously complex emotion, into which so many instincts and perceptions enter that it is scarcely analyzable at all, and is forced to go under the name of pride, was often dominant in his moods when others than his friends were before his attention. In short, Keats was as incompatible with his surroundings as ever any young poet left to the oblivion of his own society; and he was as indignant at stupidity, as tired of insignificance, as thoroughly world-weary, as a solitary enthusiast for the ideal could well be. In his last letter to George he sums the whole matter up more fully than at first but to the same purport:—

"'T is best to remain aloof from people, and like their good parts without being eternally troubled with the dull process of their every-day lives. When once a person has smoked the vapidness of the routine of society, he must either have self-interest or the love of some sort of distinction to keep him in good humor with it. All I can say is that, standing at Charing Cross and looking east, west, north, and south, I can see nothing but dullness. I hope while I am young to live retired in the country. When I grow in years and have a right to be idle, I shall enjoy cities more."

In this opinion he did retire to one place or another,—the Isle of Wight, or Winchester, or Teignmouth, and there isolating himself dreamed out his poems. He lived in a sort of ecstasy during no small portion of these solitary hours, when he could call the roaring of the wind his wife, the stars through the window panes his children, and rest contented in the abstract idea of beauty in all things. This absorption in the idea of beauty which determined the formulation of his creed in the oft-quoted lines,—

"Beauty is truth, truth beauty,—that is all
Ye know on earth, and all ye need to know;"

which also led him into that much misunderstood exclamation, "O for a life of sensations rather than of thoughts;" this intoxication, as it were, with the loveliness of earth, was in his belief a true Pythian inspiration, the medium of the divine revelation. The world takes such expressions as extravaganzas, or as mystical philosophy; but to Keats they were as commonplace as the proverbs of the hearth; he meant them as entirely lucid expressions of plain sense. This point in the criticism of Keats has been too little insisted on and brought to notice. He put his faith in the suggestions of the spirit; he relied on the intimations of what is veiled from full sight; he had little patience with minds that cannot be content with half-knowledge, or refuse to credit convictions because they cannot be expressed in detail, with logical support, and felt with the hand of sense all round, if one may employ the phrase; in other words, he believed in the imagination as a truth-finding faculty, not less valid because it presents truth in a wholly different way from the purely logical intellect. This was the deepest and most rooted persuasion of his mind from the time when he first comes under our observation. To bring together a few expressions of it is the only right way of setting forth his creed in this matter. The following extracts are from various parts of his letters, from the earliest to the later ones:—

"At once it struck me what quality went to form a man of achievement, especially in literature, and which Shakespeare possessed so enormously—I mean negative capability, that is, when a man is capable of being in uncertainties, mysteries, doubts, without any irritable reaching after fact and reason. Coleridge, for instance, would let go by a fine isolated verisimilitude caught from the penetralium of Mystery, from being incapable of remaining content with half-knowledge. This pursued through volumes would perhaps take us no further than this, that with a great poet the sense of Beauty overcomes every other consideration, or rather obliterates all consideration."

"Many a man can travel to the very bourne of heaven, and yet want confidence to put down his half-seeing."

"I never feel quite certain of any truth but from a clear perception of its beauty, and I find myself very young-minded, even in that perceptive power."

"The whole thing must, I think, have appeared to you, who are a consecutive man, as a thing almost of mere words. But I assure you that, when I wrote it, it was a regular stepping of the imagination toward a truth."

"What the imagination seizes as beauty must be truth,

whether it existed before or not . . . The imagination may be compared to Adam's dream—he awoke and found it truth. I am more zealous in this affair because I have never yet been able to perceive how anything can be known for truth by consecutive reasoning, and yet [so] it must be . . . However it may be, O for a life of sensations rather than of thoughts! It is a 'vision in the form of youth,' a shadow of reality to come."

A shadow of reality to come! What a light that sentence throws on the aspiration for sensations rather than thoughts, for beauty rather than logic, for the sight rather than the inference, for the direct rather than the mediate perception of the divine! So, at least, it is plain, Keats understood himself; and whether one counts his faith a vague self-deception, meaningless except to a mystic, or has found the most precious truth borne in upon his heart only by this selfsame way, the recognition of the poet's philosophy not merely lifts Keats out of and above the sphere of the purely sensuous, but reveals at once the spiritual substance which underlies his poetry, and which gives it vitality for all time. To other men beauty has been a passion, but to him it was a faith; it was the substance of things hoped for, the evidence of things unseen,—a shadow of the reality to come. It was not, as with other poets, in the beauty of nature, the beauty of virtue, the beauty of a woman's face, singly that he found his way to the supra-sensible; he says in his most solemn words, "I have loved the principle of beauty in all things." Dying he said it proudly, as one who had kept the faith that was given him; and since he chose that declaration as the summary of his accomplishment, it needs to be borne in mind, with all its large and many-sided meaning, by those who would pluck out the heart of his mystery.

But although to Keats the worship of beauty in all things was the essence of his life, and the delight that sprang from it the essence of his joy, he did not find in these the whole of life. At first he had been satisfied if the melancholy fit fell on him, "sudden from heaven, like a weeping cloud,"—eager to let the passion have its way with him, until it wreaked itself upon expression; but he felt this overmastering of his own will an injury, not merely exhausting but wasteful.

"Some think I have lost that poetic ardor and fire 't is said I once had; the fact is, perhaps I have; but, instead of that, I hope I shall substitute a more thoughtful and quiet power. I am more frequently, now, contented to read and think, but now and then haunted with ambitious thoughts,... scarcely content to write the best verses for the fever they leave behind. I want to compose without this fever. I hope I one day shall."

Similarly, he wishes to know more, and is determined to "get learning, get understanding," if only that he may keep his balance in the "high sensations" that draw him into their whirl.

"Although I take poetry to be the chief, there is something else wanting to one who passes his time among books and thoughts on books . . . I find earlier days are gone by—I find I can have no enjoyment in the world but continual drinking of knowledge. I find there is no worthy pursuit but the idea of doing some good to the world . . . There is but one way for me. The road lies through application, study, and thought. I will pursue it; and, for that end, purpose retiring for some years."

The years that should have perfected his powers were denied to him; his account was made up. In these broken plans, however; in this constant expansion of his view and faithful laying of his experience to heart; in the wisdom of his interpretation of what came within his scope; in a word, in his teachableness as well as in his steadier enthusiasm, his uncloyed sensibility, his finer spirituality, as the promise of Keats seems brighter, so his worth seems greater. These letters show that more had passed into his character than was ever reproduced in his poems. We come back to Lord Houghton's decision. Fine as the work of Keats is, his genius was, nevertheless,

> "The bloom, whose petals, nipt before they blew,
> Died on the promise of the fruit."

41

It has been suggested in some quarters that, notwithstanding his early death, he would probably have done no better work, if indeed he even maintained himself at the height he had reached. In support of this it is urged that Wordsworth's best poetry was written in youth, and that Coleridge's powers were employed on really excellent verse only for two years. These letters make it folly to entertain such a belief; they (and the works too) exhibit not only an increase of intellectual, but also of artistic power. No criticism of his poetry is intended here; but, in connection with this point, it may be remarked that his principal defect is in style, as is shown by the necessity he continually felt of studying literary models, which nevertheless affected his productions hardly at all, except in linguistic handling, in the choice and flow of words, after Spenser, the structure of sentences, after Milton, and later (in Lamia), after Dryden, and in a movement and kind of verbal esprit, after Ariosto. This restless change from one master to another, as well as some few critical remarks, indicates a power to form a distinctive style of his own. Again, the marked pictorial character of his poetry—the quality it has to impress one like a cartoon or a bas-relief ("the brede of marble men and maidens"), the grace of form and attitude in the figures of his poetic vision—was clearly recognized by him to be in excess in his compositions. Originally, this was due, in a high degree, to the accident of his friendship with Haydon; the portfolios of the masters helped his imagination in definiteness, in refinement, and especially in power of grouping. As the mind became more to him, and the eye less, he was dissatisfied with this trait of his works. He condemned even the most perfect composition of this kind in English: "I wish to diffuse the coloring of St. Agnes' Eve throughout a poem in which character and sentiment would be the figures to such drapery." One who could speak of such a poem as "drapery" was far from the conclusion of his artistic education. Lastly, he was from the beginning ambitious of writing dramas. Otho and King Stephen are by no means unmistakable prophecies of success, had he continued in this hope. The effort, however, proves an interest in humanity of a different order from that shown in the mythological or lyrical pieces, and makes evident how far the naturalism of his published poetry was from expressing the fullness of his mind. These three things—the incipiency of his style, the acknowledged insufficiency of picturesque art in creating the best poetry, and the ardent desire to deal with human life directly, and on the large scale, in the drama—are enough to convince us that Keats was truly a Chatterton, only less unfortunate,—"born for the future, to the future lost;" one who, though he wears, Adonis-like, the immortal youth that lies in the gift of early death, would have been even dearer to the world, had his name lost in pathos and gained in honor, as it assuredly would have done if his grass-grown grave wore the wheaten garland of England instead of the Roman daisies.

A READING IN THE
LETTERS OF JOHN KEATS

By Leon H. Nincent

One would like to know whether a first reading in the letters of Keats does not generally produce something akin to a severe mental shock. It is a sensation which presently becomes agreeable, being in that respect like a plunge into cold water, but it is undeniably a shock. Most readers of Keats, knowing him, as he should be known, by his poetry, have not the remotest conception of him as he shows himself in his letters. Hence they are unprepared for this splendid exhibition of virile intellectual health. Not that they think of him as morbid,—his poetry surely could not make this impression,—but rather that the popular conception of him is, after all these years, a legendary Keats, the poet who was killed by reviewers, the Keats of Shelley's preface to the *Adonais*, the Keats whose story is written large in the world's book of Pity and of Death. When the readers are confronted with a fair portrait of the real man, it makes them rub their eyes. Nay, more, it embarrasses them. To find themselves guilty of having pitied one who stood in small need of pity is mortifying. In plain terms, they have systematically bestowed (or have attempted to bestow) alms on a man whose income at its least was bigger than any his patrons could boast. Small wonder that now and then you find a reader, with large capacity for the sentimental, who looks back with terror to his first dip into the letters.

The legendary Keats dies hard; or perhaps we would better say that when he seems to be dying he is simply, in the good old

45

fashion of legends, taking out a new lease of life. For it is as true now as when the sentence was first penned, that 'a mixture of a lie doth ever add pleasure.' Among the many readers of good books, there will always be some whose notions of the poetical proprieties suffer greatly by the facts of Keats's history. It is so much pleasanter to them to think that the poet's sensitive spirit was wounded to death by bitter words than to know that he was carried off by pulmonary disease. But when they are tired of reading *Endymion, Isabella,* and *The Eve of St. Agnes* in the light of this incorrect conception, let them try a new reading in the light of the letters, and the masculinity of this very robust young maker of poetry will prove refreshing.

The letters are in every respect good reading. Rather than deplore their frankness, as one critic has done, we ought to rejoice in their utter want of affectation, in their boyish honesty. At every turn there is something to amuse or to startle one into thinking. We are carried back in a vivid way to the period of their composition. Not a little of the pulsing life of that time throbs anew, and we catch glimpses of notable figures. Often, the feeling is that we have been called in haste to a window to look at some celebrity passing by, and have arrived just in time to see him turn the corner. What a touch of reality, for example, does one get in reading that 'Wordsworth went rather huff'd out of town'! One is not in the habit of thinking of Wordsworth as capable of being 'huffed,' but the writer of the letters feared that he was. All of Keats's petty anxieties and small doings, as well as his aspirations and his greatest dreams, are set down here in black on white. It is a complete and charming revelation of the man. One learns how he 'went to Hazlitt's lecture on Poetry, and got there just as they were coming out;' how he was insulted at the theatre, and wouldn't tell his brothers; how it vexed him because the Irish servant said that his picture of Shakespeare looked exactly like her father, only 'her father had more color than the engraving;' how he filled in the time while waiting for the stage to start by counting the buns and tarts in

46

a pastry-cook's window, 'and had just begun on the jellies;' how indignant he was at being spoken of as 'quite the little poet;' how he sat in a hatter's shop in the Poultry while Mr. Abbey read him some extracts from Lord Byron's 'last flash poem,' *Don Juan*; how some beef was carved exactly to suit his appetite, as if he 'had been measured for it;' how he dined with Horace Smith and his brothers and some other young gentlemen of fashion, and thought them all hopelessly affected; in a word, almost anything you want to know about John Keats can be found in these letters. They are of more value than all the 'recollections' of all his friends put together. In their breezy good-nature and cheerfulness they are a fine antidote to the impression one gets of him in Haydon's account, 'lying in a white bed with a book, hectic and on his back, irritable at his weakness and wounded at the way he had been used. He seemed to be going out of life with a contempt for this world, and no hopes of the other. I told him to be calm, but he muttered that if he did not soon get better he would destroy himself.' This is taking Keats at his worst. It is well enough to know that he seemed to Haydon as Haydon has described him, but few men appear to advantage when they are desperately ill. Turn to the letters written during his tour in Scotland, when he walked twenty miles a day, climbed Ben Nevis, so fatigued himself that, as he told Fanny Keats, 'when I am asleep you might sew my nose to my great toe and trundle me around the town, like a Hoop, without waking me. Then I get so hungry a Ham goes but a very little way, and fowls are like Larks to me . . . I take a whole string of Pork Sausages down as easily as a Pen'orth of Lady's fingers.' And then he bewails the fact that when he arrives in the Highlands he will have to be contented 'with an acre or two of oaten cake, a hogshead of Milk, and a Cloaths basket of Eggs morning, noon, and night.' Here is the active Keats, of honest mundane tastes and an athletic disposition, who threatens' to cut all sick people if they do not make up their minds to cut Sickness.'

Indeed, the letters are so pleasant and amusing in the way

they exhibit minor traits, habits, prejudices, and the like, that it is a temptation to dwell upon these things. How we love a man's weaknesses—if we share them! I do not know that Keats would have given occasion for an anecdote like that told of a certain book-loving actor, whose best friend, when urged to join the chorus of praise that was quite universally sung to this actor's virtues, acquiesced by saying amiably, 'Mr. Blank undoubtedly has genius, but he can't spell;' yet there are comforting evidences that Keats was no servile follower of the 'monster Conventionality' even in his spelling, while in respect to the use of capitals he was a law unto himself. He sprinkled them through his correspondence with a lavish hand, though at times he grew so economical that, as one of his editors remarks, he would spell Romeo with a small *r*, Irishman with a small *i*, and God with a small *g*.

It is also a pleasure to find that, with his other failings, he had a touch of book-madness. There was in him the making of a first-class bibliophile. He speaks with rapture of his black-letter Chaucer, which he proposes to have bound 'in Gothique,' so as to unmodernize as much as possible its outward appearance. But to Keats books were literature or they were not literature, and one cannot think that his affections would twine about ever so bookish a volume which was merely 'curious.'

One reads with sympathetic amusement of Keats's genuine and natural horror of paying the same bill twice, 'there not being a more unpleasant thing in the world (saving a thousand and one others).' The necessity of preserving adequate evidence that a bill had been paid was uppermost in his thought quite frequently; and once when, at Leigh Hunt's instance, sundry packages of papers belonging to that eminently methodical and businesslike man of letters were to be sorted out and in part destroyed, Keats refused to burn any, 'for fear of demolishing receipts.'

But the reader will chance upon few more humorous passages than that in which the poet tells his brother George how he cures himself of the blues, and at the same time spurs his flagging powers of invention: 'Whenever I find myself growing vaporish I rouse myself, wash and put on a clean shirt, brush my hair and clothes, tie my shoe-strings neatly, and, in fact, adonize, as if I were going out—then all clean and comfortable, I sit down to write. This I find the greatest relief.' The virtues of a clean shirt have often been sung, but it remained for Keats to show what a change of linen and a general *adonizing* could do in the way of furnishing poetic stimulus. This is better than coffee, brandy, absinthe, or falling in love; and it prompts one to think anew that the English poets, taking them as a whole, were a marvelously healthy and sensible breed of men.

It is, however, in respect to the light they throw upon the poet's literary life that the letters are of highest significance. They gratify to a reasonable extent that natural desire we all have to see authorship in the act. The processes by which genius brings things to pass are so mysterious that our curiosity is continually piqued; and our failure to get at the real thing prompts us to be more or less content with mere externals. If we may not hope to see the actual process of making poetry, we may at least study the poet's manuscript. By knowing of his habits of work we flatter ourselves that we are a little nearer the secret of his power.

We must bear in mind that Keats was a boy, always a boy, and that he died before he quite got out of boyhood. To be sure, most boys of twenty-six would resent being described by so juvenile a term. But one must have successfully passed twenty-six without doing anything in particular to understand how exceedingly young twenty-six is. And to have wrought so well in so short a time, Keats must have had from the first a clear and noble conception of the nature of his work, as he must also have displayed extraordinary diligence in the doing of it. Perhaps these points are too obvious, and of a sort which would naturally occur to any one; but it will be none the less interesting to see how the letters bear witness to their truth.

In the first place, Keats was anything but a loafer at literature. He seems never to have dawdled. A fine healthiness is apparent in all allusions to his processes of work. 'I read and write about eight hours a day,' he remarks in a letter to Haydon. Bailey, Keats's Oxford friend, says that the fellow would go to his writing-desk soon after breakfast, and stay there until two or three o'clock in the afternoon. He was then writing *Endymion*. His stint was about 'fifty lines a day, . . . and he wrote with as much regularity, and apparently with as much ease, as he wrote his letters . . . Sometimes he fell short of his allotted task, but not often, and he would make it up another day. But he never forced himself.' Bailey quotes, in connection with this, Keats's own remark to the effect that poetry would better not come at all than not to come 'as naturally as the leaves of a tree.' Whether this spontaneity of production was as great as that of some other poets of his time may be questioned; but he would never have deserved Tom Nash's sneer at those writers who can only produce by 'sleeping betwixt every sentence.' Keats had in no small degree the 'fine extemporal vein' with 'invention quicker than his eye.'

We uncritically feel that it could hardly have been otherwise in the case of one with whom poetry was a passion. Keats had an infinite hunger and thirst for good poetry. His poetical life, both in the receptive and productive phases of it, was intense. Poetry was meat and drink to him. He could even urge his friend Reynolds to talk about it to him, much as one might beg a trusted friend to talk about one's lady-love, and with the confidence that only the fitting thing would be spoken. 'Whenever you write, say a word or two on some passage in Shakespeare which may have come rather new to you,'—a sentence which shows his faith in the many-sidedness of the great poetry. Shakespeare was forever 'coming new' to *him*, and he was 'haunted' by particular passages. He loved to fill the cup of his imagination with the splendors of the best poets until the cup overflowed. 'I find I cannot exist without Poetry,—without eternal Poetry; half the day will not do,—the whole of it; I began with a little, but habit has made me a leviathan.' He tells Leigh Hunt, in a letter written from Margate, that he thought so much about poetry, and 'so long together,' that he could not get to sleep at night. Whether this meant in working out ideas of his own, or living over the thoughts of other poets, is of little importance; the remark shows how deeply the roots of his life were imbedded in poetical soil. He loved a debauch in the verse of masters of his art. He could intoxicate himself with Shakespeare's sonnets. He rioted in 'all their fine things said unconsciously.' We are tempted to say, by just so much as he had large reverence for these men, by just so much he was of them.

Undoubtedly, this ability to be moved by strong imaginative work may be abused until it becomes a maudlin and quite disordered sentiment. Keats was too well balanced to be carried into appreciative excesses. He knew that mere yearning could not make a poet of one any more than mere ambition could. He understood the limits of ambition as a force in literature. Keats's ambition trembled in the presence of Keats's conception of the magnitude of the poetic office. 'I have asked myself so often why I should be a poet more than other men, seeing how great a thing it is.' Yet he had honest confidence. One cannot help liking him for the fine audacity with which he pronounces his own work good,—better even than that of a certain other great name in English literature; one cannot help loving him for the sweet humility with which he accepts the view that, after all, success or failure lies entirely without the range of self-choosing. There is a point of view from which it is folly to hold a poet responsible even for his own poetry, and when *Endymion* was spoken of as 'slipshod' Keats could reply, 'That it is so is no fault of mine . . . The Genius of Poetry must work out its own salvation in a man . . . That which is creative must create itself. In *Endymion* I leaped headlong into the sea, and thereby have become better acquainted with the soundings, the quicksands, and the rocks, than if I had stayed upon the green shore, and piped a silly pipe, and took tea and comfortable advice. I was never afraid of failure; for I would sooner fail than not be among the greatest.'

51

Well might a man who could write that last sentence look upon poetry not only as a responsible, but as a dangerous pursuit. Men who aspire to be poets are gamblers. In all the lotteries of the literary life none is so uncertain as this. A million chances that you don't win the prize to one chance that you do. It is a curious thing that ever so thoughtful and conscientious an author may not know whether he is making literature or merely writing verse. He conforms to all the canons of taste in his own day; he is devout and reverent; he shuns excesses of diction, and he courts originality; his verse seems to himself and to his unflattering friends instinct with the spirit of his time, but twenty years later it is old-fashioned. Keats, with all his feeling of certainty, stood with head uncovered before that power which gives poetical gifts to one, and withholds them from another. Above all would he avoid self-delusion in these things. 'There is no greater Sin after the seven deadly than to flatter one's self into an idea of being a great Poet.'

Keats, if one may judge from a letter written to John Taylor in February, 1818, had little expectation that his *Endymion* was going to be met with universal plaudits. He doubtless looked for fair treatment. He probably had no thought of being sneeringly addressed as 'Johnny,' or of getting recommendations to return to his 'plasters, pills, and ointment boxes.' In fact, he looked upon the issue as entirely problematical. He seemed willing to take it for granted that in *Endymion* he had but moved into the go-cart from the leading-strings. 'If *Endymion* serves me for a pioneer, perhaps I ought to be content, for thank God I can read and perhaps understand Shakespeare to his depths; and I have, I am sure, many friends who if I fail will attribute any change in my life to humbleness rather than pride,—to a cowering under the wings of great poets rather than to bitterness that I am not appreciated.' And for evidence of any especial bitterness because of the lashing he received one will search the letters in vain. Keats was manly and good-humored, most of his morbidity being referred directly to his ill health. The trouncing he had at the hands of the reviewers was no more violent than the one administered to Tennyson by Professor Wilson. Critics, good and bad, can do much harm. They may terrorize a timid spirit. But a greater terror than the fear of the reviewers hung over the head of John Keats. He stood in awe of his own artistic and poetic sense. He could say with truth that his own domestic criticism had given him pain without comparison beyond what *Blackwood* or the *Quarterly* could possibly inflict. If he had had any terrible heart-burning over their malignancy, if he had felt that his life was poisoned, he could hardly have forborne some allusion to it in his letters to his brother, George Keats. But he is almost imperturbable. He talks of the episode freely, says that he has been urged to publish his *Pot of Basil* as a reply to the reviewers, has no idea that he can be made ridiculous by abuse, notes the futility of attacks of this kind, and then, with a serene conviction that is irresistible, adds, 'I think I shall be among the English Poets after my death!'

Such egoism of genius is magnificent; the more so as it appears in Keats because it runs parallel with deep humility in the presence of the masters of his art. Naturally, the masters who were in their graves were the ones he reverenced the most and read without stint. But it was by no means essential that a poet be a dead poet before Keats did him homage. It is impossible to think that Keats's attitude towards Wordsworth was other than finely appreciative, in spite of the fact that he applauded Reynolds's *Peter Bell*, and inquired almost petulantly why one should be teased with Wordsworth's 'Matthew with a bough of wilding in his hand.' But it is also impossible that his sense of humor should not have been aroused by much that he found in Wordsworth. It was Wordsworth he meant when he said, 'Every man has his speculations, but every man does not brood and peacock over them till he makes a false coinage and deceives himself,'—a sentence, by the way, quite as unconsciously funny as some of the things he laughed at in the works of his great contemporary.

It will be pertinent to quote here two or three of the good critical words which Keats scattered through his letters. Emphasizing the use of simple means in his art, he says, 'I think that poetry should surprise by a fine excess, and not by singularity; it should strike the reader as a wording of his own highest thoughts, and appear almost a remembrance.'

'We hate poetry that has a palpable design upon us . . . Poetry should be great and unobtrusive, a thing which enters into one's soul, and does not startle it or amaze it with itself, but with its subject.' Or as Ruskin has put the thing with respect to painting, 'Entirely first-rate work is so quiet and natural that there can be no dispute over it.'

Keats appears to have been in no sense a hermit. With the exception of Byron, he was perhaps less of a recluse than any of his poetical contemporaries. With respect to society he frequently practiced total abstinence; but the world was amusing, and he liked it. He was fond of the theatre, fond of whist, fond of visiting the studios, fond of going to the houses of his friends. But he would run no risks; he was shy and he was proud. He dreaded contact with the ultra-fashionables. Naturally, his opportunities for such intercourse were limited, but he cheerfully neglected his opportunities. I doubt if he ever bewailed his humble origin; nevertheless, the constitution of English society would hardly admit of his forgetting it. He had that pardonable pride which will not allow a man to place himself among those who, though outwardly fair-spoken, offer the insult of a hostile and patronizing mental attitude.

Most of his friendships were with men, and this is to his credit. The man is spiritually warped who is incapable of a deep and abiding friendship with one of his own sex; and to go a step farther, that man is utterly to be distrusted whose only friends are among women. We may not be prepared to accept the radical position of a certain young thinker, who proclaims, in season, but defiantly, that 'men are the idealists, after all;' yet it is easy to comprehend how one may take this point of view.

The friendships of men are a vastly more interesting and poetic study than the friendships of men and women. This is in the nature of the case. It is the usual victory of the normal over the abnormal. As a rule, it is impossible for a friendship to exist between a man and woman, unless the man and woman in question be husband and wife. Then it is as rare as it is beautiful. And with men, the most admirable spectacle is not always that where attendant circumstances prompt to heroic display of friendship, for it is often so much easier to die than to live. But you may see young men pledging their mutual love and support in this difficult and adventurous quest of what is noblest in the art of living. Such love will not urge to a theatrical posing, and it can hardly find expression in words. Words seem to profane it. I do not say that Keats stood in such an ideal relation to any one of his many friends whose names appear in the letters. He gave of himself to them all, and he received much from each. No man of taste and genius could have been other than flattered by the way in which Keats approached him. He was charming in his attitude toward Haydon; and when Haydon proposed sending Keats's sonnet to Wordsworth, the young poet wrote, 'The Idea of your sending it to Wordsworth put me out of breath—you know with what Reverence I would send my well wishes to him.'

But interesting as a chapter on Keats's friendships with men would be, we are bound to confess that in dramatic intensity it would grow pale when laid beside that fiery love passage of his life, his acquaintance with Fanny Brawne. The thirty-nine letters given in the fourth volume of Buxton Forman's edition of *Keats's Works* tell the story of this affair of a poet's heart. These are the letters which Mr. William Watson says he has never read, and at which no consideration shall ever induce him to look. But Mr. Watson reflects upon people who have been human enough to read them when he compares such a proceeding on his own part (were he able to be guilty of it) to the indelicacy of 'listening at a keyhole or spying over a wall.' This is not a just illustration. The man who takes upon himself the responsibility of being the first to open such intimate letters, and adds thereto the infinitely greater responsibility of publishing them in so attractive a form that he who runs will stop running in order to read,—such an editor will need to satisfy Mr. Watson that in so doing he was not listening at a keyhole or spying over a wall. For the general public, the wall is down, and the door containing the keyhole thrown open. Perhaps our duty is not to look. I, for one, wish that great men would not leave their love letters around. Nay, I wish you a better wish than that: it is that the perfect taste of the gentleman and scholar who gave us in its present form the correspondence of Carlyle and Emerson, the early and later letters of Carlyle, and the letters of Lowell might have control of the private papers of every man of genius whose teachings the world holds dear. He would need for this an indefinite lease upon life; but since I am wishing, let me wish largely. There is need of such wishing. Many editors have been called, and only two or three chosen.

But why one who reads the letters of Keats to Fanny Brawne should have any other feeling than that of pity for a poor fellow who was so desperately in love as to be wretched because of it I do not see. Even a cynic will grant that Keats was not disgraced, since it is very clear that he did not yield readily to what Dr. Holmes calls the great passion. He had a complacent boyish superiority of attitude with respect to all those who are weak enough to love women. 'Nothing,' he says, 'strikes me so forcibly with a sense of the ridiculous as love. A man in love I do think cuts the sorryest figure in the world. Even when I know a poor fool to be really in pain about it I could burst out laughing in his face. His pathetic visage becomes irresistible.' Then he speaks of that dinner party of stutterers and squinters described in the *Spectator*, and says that it would please him more 'to scrape together a party of lovers.' If this letter be genuine and the date of it correctly given, it was written three months after he had succumbed to the attractions of Fanny Brawne. Perhaps he was trying to brave it out, as one may laugh to conceal embarrassment.

In a much earlier letter than this he hopes he shall never marry, but nevertheless has a good deal to say about a young lady with fine eyes and fine manners and a 'rich Eastern look.' He discovers that he can talk to her without being uncomfortable or ill at ease. 'I am too much occupied in admiring to be awkward or in a tremble . . . She kept me awake one night as a tune of Mozart's might do . . . I don't cry to take the moon home with me in my pocket, nor do I fret to leave her behind me.' But he was not a little touched, and found it easy to fill two pages on the subject of this dark beauty. She was a friend of the Reynolds family. She crosses the stage of the Keats drama in a very impressive manner, and then disappears.

The most extraordinary passage to be met with in relation to the poet's attitude towards women is in a letter written to Benjamin Bailey in July, 1818. As a partial hint towards its full meaning I would take two phrases in *Daniel Deronda*. George Eliot says of Gwendolen Harleth that there was 'a certain fierceness of maidenhood in her,' which expression is quoted here only to emphasize the girl's feeling towards men as described a little later, when Rex Gascoigne attempted to tell her his love. Gwendolen repulsed him with a sort of fury that was surprising to herself. The author's interpretative comment is, '*The life of passion had begun negatively in her.*'

So one might say of Keats that the life of passion began negatively in him. He was conscious of a hostility of temper towards women. 'I am certain I have not a right feeling toward women—at this moment I am striving to be just to them, but I cannot.' He certainly started with a preposterously high ideal, for he says that when a schoolboy he thought a fair woman a pure goddess. And now he is disappointed at finding women only the equals of men. This disappointment helps to give rise to that antagonism which is almost inexplicable save as George Eliot's phrase throws light upon it. He thinks that he insults women by these perverse feelings of unprovoked hostility. 'Is it not extraordinary,' he exclaims, 'when among men I have no evil thoughts, no malice, no spleen; I feel free to speak or to be silent; . . . I am free from all suspicion, and comfortable. When I am among women, I have evil thoughts, malice, spleen; I cannot speak or be silent; I am full of suspicions, and therefore listen to nothing; I am in a hurry to be gone.' He wonders how this trouble is to be cured. He speaks of it as a prejudice produced from 'a gordian complication of feelings, which must take time to unravel.' And then, with a good-humored, characteristic touch, he drops the subject, saying, 'After all, I do think better of women than to suppose they care whether Mister John Keats, five feet high, likes them or not.'

Three or four months after writing these words he must have begun his friendly relations with the Brawne family. This would be in October or November, 1818. Keats's description of Fanny is hardly flattering, and not even vivid. What is one to make of the colorless expression 'a fine style of countenance of the lengthened sort'? But she was fair to him, and any beauty beyond that would have been superfluous. We look at the silhouette and sigh in vain for trace of the loveliness which ensnared Keats. But if our daguerreotypes of forty years ago can so entirely fail of giving one line of that which in its day passed for dazzling beauty, let us not be unreasonable in our demands upon the artistic capabilities of a silhouette. Not infrequently is it true that the style of dress seems to disfigure. But we have learned, in course of experience, that pretty women manage to be pretty, however much fashion, with their cordial help, disguises them.

It is easy to see from the letters that Keats was a difficult lover. Hard to please at the best, his two sicknesses, one of body and one of heart, made him whimsical. Nothing less than a woman of genius could possibly have managed him. He was jealous, perhaps quite unreasonably so. Fanny Brawne was young, a bit coquettish, buoyant, and he misinterpreted her vivacity. She liked what is commonly called 'the world,' and so did he when he was well; but looking through the discolored glass of ill health, all nature was out of harmony. For these reasons it happens that the letters at times come very near to being documents in love-madness. Many a line in them gives sharp pain, as a record of heart-suffering must always do. You may read Richard Steele's love letters for pleasure, and have it. The love letters of Keats scorch and sting; and the worst of it is that you cannot avoid reflecting upon the transitory character of such a passion. Withering young love like this does not last. It may burn itself out, or, what is quite as likely, it may become sober and rational. But in its earlier maddened state it cannot possibly last; a man would die under it. Men as a rule do not so die, for the race of the Azra is nearly extinct.

These Brawne letters, however, are not without their bright side; and it is wonderful to see how Keats's elastic nature would rebound the instant that the pressure of the disease relaxed. He is at times almost gay. The singing of a thrush prompts him to talk in his natural epistolary voice: 'There's the Thrush again—I can't afford it—he'll run me up a pretty Bill for Music—besides he ought to know I deal at Clementi's.' And in the letter which he wrote to Mrs. Brawne from Naples is a touch of the old bantering Keats when he says that 'it's misery to have an intellect in splints.' He was never strong enough to write again to Fanny, or even to read her letters.

I should like to close this reading with a few sentences from a letter written to Reynolds in February, 1818. Keats says: 'I had an idea that a man might pass a very pleasant life in this manner— let him on a certain day read a certain Page of full Poesy or distilled Prose, and let him wander with it, and muse upon it, . . . and prophesy upon it, and dream upon it, until it becomes stale—but when will it do so? Never! When Man has arrived at a certain ripeness in intellect any one grand and spiritual passage serves him as a starting post towards all the "two-and-thirty Palaces." How happy is such a voyage of conception, what delicious diligent Indolence! . . . Nor will this sparing touch of noble Books be any irreverence to their Writers—for perhaps the honors paid by Man to Man are trifles in comparison to the Benefit done by great Works to the Spirit and pulse of good by their mere passive existence.'

May we not say that the final test of great literature is that it be able to be read in the manner here indicated? As Keats read, so did he write. His own work was

> 'accomplished in repose
> Too great for haste, too high for rivalry.'

KEATS

By Barnette Miller

It was about the year 1815 that Keats showed to his former school friend, Charles Cowden Clarke, the following sonnet, the first indication the latter had that Keats had written poetry:

> "What though, for showing truth to flatter'd state,
> Kind Hunt was shut in prison, yet has he,
> In his immortal spirit been as free
> As the sky-searching lark, and as elate.
> Minion of grandeur! think you he did wait?
> Think you he nought but prison walls did see,
> Till, so unwilling thou unturn'dst the key?
> Ah, no! far happier, nobler was his fate!
> In Spenser's halls he stray'd, and bowers fair,
> Culling enchanted flowers; and he flew
> With daring Milton through the fields of air:
> To regions of his own his genius true
> Took happy flights. Who shall his fame impair
> When thou art dead, and all thy wretched crew?"

This admiration, expressed before Keats had met Hunt, was due to the influence of the Clarke family and to Keats's acquaintance with *The Examiner*, which he saw regularly during his school days at Enfield and which he continued to borrow from Clarke during his medical apprenticeship. Clarke later showed to Leigh Hunt two or three of Keats's poems. Of the reception of one of them (*How Many Bards Gild the Lapses*

61

of Time) Clarke said:

"I could not but anticipate that Hunt would speak encouragingly, and indeed approvingly, of the compositions— written, too, by a youth under age; but my partial spirit was not prepared for the unhesitating and prompt admiration which broke forth before he had read twenty lines of the first poem."

Hunt invited Keats to visit him. Of this first meeting between the two men, Clarke wrote:

"That was a red letter day in the young poet's life, and one which will never fade with me while memory lasts. The character and expression of Keats's features would arrest even the casual passenger in the street; and now they were wrought to a tone of animation that I could not but watch with interest, knowing what was in store for him from the bland encouragement, and Spartan deference in attention, with fascinating conversational eloquence, that he was to encounter and receive . . . The interview, which stretched into three 'morning calls', was the prelude to many after-scenes and saunterings about Caen Wood and its neighborhood; for Keats was suddenly made a familiar of the household, and was always welcomed."

Hunt's account of the meeting is as follows:

"I shall never forget the impression made upon me by the exuberant specimens of genuine though young poetry that were laid before me, and the promise of which was seconded by the fine fervid countenance of the writer. We became intimate on the spot, and I found the young poet's heart as warm as his imagination. We read and we walked together, and used to write verse of an evening upon a given subject. No imaginative pleasure was left untouched by us, or unenjoyed; from the recollections of the bards and patriots of old, to the luxury of a summer rain at our window, or the clicking of the coal in the winter-time. Not long afterwards, having the pleasure of entertaining at dinner Mr. Godwin, Mr. Hazlitt, and Mr. Basil Montagu, I showed the verses of my young friend, and they were pronounced to be as extraordinary as I thought them."

Leigh Hunt discovered Keats, by no means a small thing, for as he himself has said: "To admire and comment upon the genius that two or three hundred years have applauded, and to discover what will partake of applause two or three hundred years hence, are processes of a very different description." With the same power of prophetic discernment, writing in 1828, he realized to the full the greatness of Keats and predicted that growth of his fame in the future which has since taken place. Keats's account of his reception is given in the sonnet *Keen fitful gusts are whisp'ring here and there*:

"For I am brimfull of the friendliness
That in a little cottage I have found;
Of fair hair'd Milton's eloquent distress,
And all his love for gentle Lycid drown'd;
Of lovely Laura in her light green dress,
And faithful Petrarch gloriously crowned."

The date of the introduction of Keats to Hunt has been placed variously from November, 1815, to the end of the year 1816. He says:

"It was not at Hampstead that I first saw Keats. It was in York Buildings, in the New Road (No. 8), where I wrote part of the *Indicator*—and he resided with me while in Mortimer Terrace, Kentish Town (No. 13), where I concluded it. I mention this for the curious in such things, among whom I am one."

If this statement were correct, it would make the meeting about two or three years later than has generally been supposed, for Leigh Hunt did not move to York Buildings until 1818, and he did not begin work on the *Indicator* until October, 1819. Clarke states positively that the meeting took place at Hampstead. From this evidence Mr. Colvin has suggested the early spring of 1816 as the most probable date. What seems better evidence than any that has yet been brought forward is a passage in *The Examiner* of June 1, 1817, in Hunt's review of Keats's *Poems* of

1817, where he says that the poet is a personal friend whom he announced to the public a short time ago (this allusion can only be to an article in *The Examiner* of December 1, 1816) and that the friendship dates from "no greater distance of time than the announcement above mentioned. We had published one of his sonnets in our paper, without knowing more of him than of any other anonymous correspondent; but at the period in question a friend brought us one morning some copies in verse, which he said were from the pen of a youth . . . We had not read more than a dozen lines when we recognized a young poet indeed." This seems conclusive evidence that the meeting did not take place until the winter of 1816, for Hunt's testimony written in 1817, when the circumstance was fresh in his mind is certainly more trustworthy than his impression of it at the time that he revised his *Autobiography* in 1859 at the age of seventy-five years.

The two men, before they came in contact, had much in common, and Hunt's influence, while in some cases an inspiring force, more often fostered instincts already existing in Keats. Both possessed by nature a deep love of poetry, color and melody, and both "were given to 'luxuriating' somewhat voluptuously over the 'deliciousness' of the beautiful in art, books or nature." At the very beginning of their acquaintance, notwithstanding a disparity in age of eleven years, they were wonderfully drawn to each other. Spenser was their favorite poet. Both had a great love for Chaucer, for Oriental fable and for Chivalric romance, and an unusual knowledge of Greek myth. But even at the height of their intimacy, the friendship seems to have remained more intellectual than personal, a fact due no doubt to Keats's reserve and Hunt's "incuriousness." Except for this drawback Hunt considered the friendship ideal. He says: "Mr. Keats and I were old friends of the old stamp, between whom there was no such thing as obligation, except the pleasure of it. He enjoyed the privilege of greatness with all whom he knew, rendering it delightful to be obliged by him, and an equal, but not a greater delight, to oblige. It was a pleasure to his friends to have him in their houses, and he did not grude it."

Through Hunt, Keats was introduced to a circle of literary men whose companionship was an important factor in his development, notably Haydon, Godwin, Hazlitt, Shelley, Vincent Novello, Horace Smith, Cornelius Webbe, Basil Montagu, the Olliers, Barry Cornwall, and later Wordsworth.

For about a year following the meeting of the two, Hunt undoubtedly exerted the strongest influence of any living man over the young poet. Severn said that Keats's introduction to Hunt wrought a great change in him and "intoxicated him with an excess of enthusiasm which kept by him four or five years." Mr. Forman says that "Charles Cowden Clarke, as his early mentor, Leigh Hunt and Haydon as his most powerful encouragers at the important epoch of adolescence, must be credited with much of the active influence that took Keats out of the path to a medical practitioner's life, and set his feet in the devious paths of literature." Keats's interest in his profession had decreased as his knowledge and love of poetry grew. With the publication of his *Poems* in 1817, and his retirement in April of that year from London to the Isle of Wight "to be alone and improve" himself and to continue *Endymion*, his decision was finally made in favor of a literary life. Hunt's aid at this time took the practical form of publishing Keats's poems in *The Examiner* and of drawing the attention of the public to them by comments and reviews. Whether he ever paid Keats for any of his contributions to his periodicals is not known. Through the influence of Hunt the Ollier brothers were induced to undertake the publication of Keats's first volume of poems.

It is dedicated to Leigh Hunt in the sonnet *Glory and loveliness have passed away.*

The sestet refers directly to him:

"But there are left delights as high as these,
And I shall ever bless my destiny,
That in a time, when under pleasant trees
Pan is no longer sought, I feel a free
A leafy luxury, seeing I could please
With these poor offerings, a man like thee."

Hunt replied in the sonnet *To John Keats*, quoted here in full because of its inacessibility:

"'Tis well you think me truly one of those,
Whose sense discerns the loveliness of things;
For surely as I feel the bird that sings
Behind the leaves, or dawn as it up grows,
Or the rich bee rejoicing as he goes,
Or the glad issue of emerging springs,
Or overhead the glide of a dove's wings,
Or turf, or trees, or midst of all, repose.
And surely as I feel things lovelier still,
The human look, and the harmonious form
Containing woman, and the smile in ill,
And such a heart as Charles's wise and warm,—
As surely as all this, I see ev'n now,
Young Keats, a flowering laurel on your brow."

In 1820, Hunt dedicated his translation of Tasso's *Aminta* to Keats.

In spite of a eulogistic article by Hunt running in *The Examiners* of June 1, July 6 and 13, 1817, and other notices in some of the provincial papers, the *Poems* sold not very well at first, and later, not at all. Praise from the editor of *The Examiner*, although offered with the kindest intentions in the world, was about the worst thing that could possibly have happened to Keats, for, politically and poetically, Leigh Hunt was most unpopular at this time; and it was noised abroad that Keats too was a radical in politics and in religion, a disciple of the apostate in his attack on the established and accepted creed of poetry. As a matter of fact, Keats's interest in politics decreased as his knowledge of poetry increased, although, "as a party-badge and sign of ultra-liberalism," he, like Hunt, Byron and Shelley continued to wear the soft turn-down collars in contrast to the stiff collars and enormous cravats of the time. In religion Keats vented his dislike of sect and creed on the Kirk of Scotland, as Hunt had on the Methodists. His "simply-sensuous Beauty-worship" Palgrave attributes to the "moral laxity" of Hunt. Unless Palgrave, like Haydon, refers to Hunt's unorthodoxy in matters of church and state, it is difficult to understand on what evidence he bases this statement; in the first place, a charge of moral laxity is not borne out by the recorded facts of Hunt's life, but only by such untrustworthy tradition as still lingers in the public mind from the Cockney School articles of *Blackwood's* and the *Quarterly*. Carlyle said that he was of "most exemplary private deportment." Byron, Shelley and Lamb testified to his virtuous life. In the second place, a close comparison of the works of the two now leads one to conclude that "simply-sensuous Beauty-worship" existed to a much higher degree in Keats than in Hunt, and that so strong an innate tendency would have developed without outward stimulus from any one. While both men sought the good and worshipped the beautiful, Keats, unlike Hunt, recognized somewhat "the burthen and the mystery" of human life.

Keats, during his stay in the Isle of Wight and a visit to Oxford with Bailey in the spring and summer of 1817, worked on *Endymion*, finishing it in the fall. The letters exchanged between him and Hunt during his absence were friendly, but a feeling of coolness began before his return. In a letter from Margate May 10, 1817, there is a curiously obscure reference to the *Nymphs*:

"How have you got on among them? How are the *Nymphs*? I suppose they have led you a fine dance. Where are you now?—in Judea, Cappadocia, or the parts of Lybia about Cyrene? Stranger from 'Heaven, Hues, and Prototypes' I wager you have given several new turns to the old saying, 'Now the maid was fair and pleasant to look on,' as well as made a little variation in 'Once upon a time.' Perhaps, too, you have rather varied, 'Here endeth the first lesson.' Thus I hope you have made a horseshoe business of 'unsuperfluous life,' 'faint bowers' and fibrous roots."

A letter written by Haydon to Keats, dated May 11, 1817, warned Keats against Hunt, and, with others of its kind, was possibly the insidious beginning of the coolness which followed: "Beware, for God's sake of the delusions and sophistications that are ripping up the talents and morality of our friend! He will go out of the world the victim of his own weakness and the dupe of his own self-delusions, with the contempt of his enemies and the sorrow of his friends, and the cause he undertook to support injured by his own neglect of character." A letter in reply from Keats, written the day after he wrote the passage about the *Nymphs*, accounts for its dissembling tone:

"I wrote to Hunt yesterday—scarcely know what I said in it. I could not talk about Poetry in the way I should have liked for I was not in humour with either his or mine. His self delusions are very lamentable—they have inticed him into a Situation which I should be less eager after than that of a galley Slave,—what you observe thereon is very true must be in time [sic].

Perhaps it is a self delusion to say so—but I think I could not be deceived in the manner that Hunt is—may I die to-morrow if I am to be. There is no greater Sin after the seven deadly than to flatter oneself into the idea of being a great Poet . . . "

To judge from the testimony of his brother George it is not surprising that Keats succumbed to Haydon's influence against Hunt: "his nervous, morbid temperament led him to misconstrue the motives of his best friends." In the last days of his life, his suspicion and bitterness were general. In a letter to Bailey, June, 1818, Keats says: "I have suspected everybody." January, 1820, he wrote Georgiana Keats, "Upon the whole I dislike mankind." Haydon may have sincerely believed Hunt's influence to be injurious because of the latter's unorthodoxy in matters of religion. He wrote that Keats "could not bring his mind to bear on one object, and was at the mercy of every petty theory that Leigh Hunt's ingenuity would suggest . . . He had a tendency to religion when I first knew him, but Leigh Hunt soon forced it from his mind . . . Leigh Hunt was the unhinger of his best dispositions. Latterly, Keats saw Leigh Hunt's weaknesses. I distrusted his leader, but Keats would not cease to visit him, because he thought Hunt ill-used. This shows Keats's goodness of heart." It is not to be regretted that Haydon lessened Keats's estimate of Hunt's literary infallibility, for his influence was most injurious in that direction; but it is to be regretted that he impugned a friendship in which Hunt was certainly sincere and by which Keats had benefited.

In September, just before Keats's return, he seems somewhat mollified and writes to John Hamilton Reynolds of Leigh Hunt's pleasant companionship; he has failings, "but then his make-ups are very good."

On his return to Hampstead in October, 1817, Keats found affairs among the circle in a very bad way.

Everybody "seems at Loggerheads—There's Hunt infatuated—there's Haydon's picture in statu quo—There's Hunt walks up and down his painting room—criticising every head most unmercifully. There's Horace Smith tired of Hunt. 'The web of our life is of mingled yarn.' . . . I am quite disgusted with literary men and will never know another except Wordsworth—no not even Byron. Here is an instance of the friendship of such. Haydon and Hunt have known each other many years . . . Haydon says to me, Keats, don't show your lines to Hunt on any Account or he will have done half for you—so it appears Hunt wishes it to be thought. When he met Reynolds in the Theatre, John told him that I was getting on to the completion of 4,000 lines—Ah! says Hunt, had it not been for me they would have been 7,000! If he will say this to Reynolds, what would he to other people? Haydon received a Letter a little while back on this subject from some Lady—which contains a caution to me, thro' him, on the subject—now is not all this a most paultry (sic) thing to think about?"

Hunt had tried to persuade Keats not to write a long poem. Keats wrote of this: "Hunt's dissuasion was of no avail—I refused to visit Shelley that I might have my own unfettered scope; and after all, I shall have the reputation of Hunt's élève. His corrections and amputations will by the knowing ones be traced in the poem."

During 1818, Leigh Hunt in his critical w 'To put a spirit of youth in everythin ork remained silent concerning Keats, probably because of his sincere disapproval of *Endymion* and secondly, because he realized that his praise would be injurious. The attacks on Hunt in *Blackwood's* and the *Quarterly* had foreshadowed an attack of the same virulent kind on Keats. The realization came with the publication of *Endymion*. The article on "Johnny Keats," fourth of the series on the Cockney School in *Blackwood's Magazine*, appeared almost simultaneously with his return from Scotland, and the one in the *Quarterly* in September of the same year. These will be discussed in a later chapter. Suspicions of neglect on the part of Hunt murmured in Keats's mind like a discordant undertone, although the friendship continued as warm as ever on Hunt's part. Keats was passive, without, however, the old sense of dependence and trust. December 28, 1817, he writes to his brothers of the "drivelling egotism" of *The Examiner* article on the obsoletion of Christmas gambols and pastimes. In a journal letter written to George Keats and his wife in Louisville during December and January, 1819, the old liking has become almost repugnance: "Hunt keeps on in his old way—I am completely tired of it all. He has lately published a Pocket Book called the literary Pocket-Book—full of the most sickening stuff you can imagine"; yet Keats suffered himself to become a contributor to this same book with two sonnets, *The Human Seasons* and *To Ailsa Rock*. Again in the same letter:

"The night we went to Novello's there was a complete set-to of Mozart and punning. I was so completely tired of it that if I were to follow my own inclinations I should never meet any of that set again, not even Hunt who is certainly a pleasant fellow in the main when you are with him, but in reality he is vain, egotistical, and disgusting in matters of taste and morals. He understands many a beautiful thing; but then, instead of giving other minds credit for the same degree of perception as he himself possesses,—he begins an explanation in such a curious manner that our taste and self-love is offended continually. Hunt does one harm by making fine things petty and beautiful things hateful. Through him I am indifferent to Mozart, I care not for white Busts—and many a glorious thing when associated with him becomes a nothing."

Continuing in the same strain:

"I will have no more Wordsworth or Hunt in particular. Why should we be of the tribe of Manasseh when we can wander with Esau? Why should we kick against the Pricks, when we can walk on Roses? . . . I don't mean to deny Wordsworth's grandeur and Hunt's merit, but I mean to say that we need not to be teazed with grandeur and merit, when we can have them uncontaminated and unobtrusive. Let us have the old Poets and Robin Hood."

And again:

"Hunt has damned Hampstead and masks and sonnets and Italian tales. Wordsworth has damned the lakes—Milman has damned the old drama—West has damned wholesale. Peacock has damned satire—Ollier has damned Music—Hazlitt has damned the bigoted and the blue-stockinged; how durst the Man?!"

A parody on the conversation of Hunt's set, in which he is the principal actor, carries with it a ridicule that is unkinder than the bitterness of dislike, and difficult to reconcile with the fact that Keats at the same time preserved the semblance of friendship.

"Scene, a little Parlour—Enter Hunt—Gattie—Hazlitt—Mrs. Novello—Ollier. *Gattie*:—Ha! Hunt got into your new house? Ha! Mrs. Novello: seen Altam and his wife? *Mrs. N*.: Yes (with a grin) it's Mr. Hunt's isn't it? *Gattie*: Hunt's? no, ha! Mr. Ollier, I congratulate you upon the highest compliment I ever heard paid to the Book. Mr. Hazlitt, I hope you are well. *Hazlitt*:— Yes Sir, no Sir—*Mr. Hunt* (at the Music) 'La Biondina' etc. Hazlitt, did you ever hear this?—"La Biondina" &c. *Hazlitt*: O no Sir—I never—*Ollier*:—Do Hunt give it us over again— divine—*Gattie*:—divino—Hunt when does your Pocket-Book come out—*Hunt*:—'What is this absorbs me quite?' O we are spinning on a little, we shall floridize soon I hope. Such a thing was very much wanting—people think of nothing but money getting—now for me I am rather inclined to the liberal side of things. I am reckoned lax in my Christian principles, etc., etc., etc., etc."

Such a dual attitude in Keats can be explained only by a dual feeling in his mind, for it is impossible to believe him capable of deliberate deceit. He may have realized Hunt's affectation and superficiality and "disgusting taste"; he was probably swayed by Haydon to distrust Hunt's morals; the suspicions planted by Haydon concerning *Endymion* rankled; but at the same time Hunt's charm of personality, and the assistance and encouragement given in the first days of their friendship, formed a bond difficult to break. Of Leigh Hunt's attitude there can be no doubt, for through his long life of more than threescore years and ten, filled with many friendships of many kinds, he can in no instance be charged with insincerity. There is no conclusive proof on record to show him deserving of the insinuations which Keats believed in respect to *Endymion*, for Haydon is not trustworthy, and the opinion of a lady given through Haydon may be dismissed on the same grounds. Reynolds' testimony is not damaging in itself, and in the absence of facts to the contrary may have been wrongly construed by Keats. To the charges against himself, Leigh Hunt has replied in the following passage, "affecting and persuasive in its unrestrained pathos of remonstrance":

"an irritable morbidity appears even to have driven his suspicions to excess; and this not only with regard to the acquaintance whom he might reasonably suppose to have had some advantages over him, but to myself, who had none; for I learned the other day, with extreme pain, such as I am sure so kind and reflecting a man as Mr. Monckton Milnes would not have inflicted on me could he have foreseen it, that Keats at one period of his intercourse suspected Shelley and myself of a wish to see him undervalued! Such are the tricks which constant infelicity can play with the most noble natures. For Shelley, let *Adonais* answer. For myself, let every word answer which I uttered about him, living and dead, and such as I now proceed to repeat. I might as well have been told that I wished to see the flowers or the stars undervalued, or my own heart that loved him."

Hunt's feeling towards Keats is nowhere better expressed than in his *Autobiography*: "I could not love him as deeply as I did Shelley. That was impossible. But my affection was only second to the one which I entertained for that heart of hearts."

Keats's atonement is contained in the last letter that he ever wrote: "If I recover, I will do all in my power to correct the mistakes made during sickness, and if I should not, all my faults will be forgiven."

Haydon's influence over Keats was at its height in 1817 and 1818. His gifts and his enthusiasm, his "fresh magnificence" carried Keats by storm. It was not until about July 1818 that a reaction against Haydon in favor of Hunt set in, brought about by money transactions between Keats and Haydon, and the indifference of the latter in repaying a debt when he knew Keats's necessity. Keats probably never ceased to feel that Hunt's influence as a poet had been injurious, as indeed it was, but the relative stability of his two friends adjusted itself after this experience with Haydon. Affairs seem to have been smoothed over with Hunt, and were not disturbed again until a short time before Keats's departure for Italy, when his morbid suspicions, which even led him to accuse his friend Brown of flirting with Fanny Brawne, seem to have been renewed.

In 1820, Brown, with whom Keats had been living since his brother Tom's death, went on a second tour to Scotland. Keats, unable to accompany him, took a lodging in Wesleyan Place, Kentish Town, to be near Hunt, who was living in Mortimer Street. Brown says: "It was his choice, during my absence to lodge at Kentish Town, that he might be near his friend, Leigh Hunt, in whose companionship he was ever happy." In a letter to Fanny Brawne, Keats said Hunt "amuses me very kindly." It is not likely, judging from this overture, that there had ever been an actual cessation of intercourse, notwithstanding what Keats wrote in his letters; and the act points to a revival of the old feeling on his part. About the twenty-second or twenty-third of June, 1820, Keats left his rooms and moved to Leigh Hunt's home to be nursed. He remained about seven weeks with the family, when there occurred an unfortunate incident which resulted in his abrupt departure August 12, 1820. A letter of Fanny Brawne's was delivered to him two days late with the seal broken. The contretemps was due to the misconduct of a servant, but it was interpreted by Keats as treachery on the part of the family. At the moment he would accept no explanations or apologies. He writes of this incident to Fanny Brawne:

"My friends have behaved well to me in every instance but one, and there they have become tattlers, and inquisitors into my conduct: spying upon a secret I would rather die than share it with anybody's confidence. For this I cannot wish them well, I care not to see any of them again. If I am the Theme, I will not be the Friend of idle Gossips. Good gods what a shame it is our Loves should be put into the microscope of a Coterie. Their laughs should not affect you (I may perhaps give you reasons some day for these laughs, for I suspect a few people to hate me well enough, *for reasons I know of,* who have pretended a great friendship for me) when in competition with one, who if he should never see you again would make you the Saint of his memory. These Laughers, who do not like you, who envy you for your Beauty, who would have God-bless'd me from you for ever: who were plying me with disencouragements with respect to you eternally. People are revengeful—do not mind them—do nothing but love me."

In his next letter to her he says:

"I shall never be able to endure any more the society of any of those who used to meet at Elm Cottage and Wentworth Place. The last two years taste like brass upon my Palate."

The lack of self-control and the distrust seen in these extracts show that Keats was laboring under hallucinations produced by an ill mind and body; the letters from which they have been taken are unnatural, almost terrible, in their passion and rebellion against fate.

Keats moved to the residence of the Brawnes. While he was here the trouble seems to have been smoothed over, for in a letter to Hunt he says: "You will be glad to hear I am going to delay a little at Mrs. Brawne's. I hope to see you whenever you get time, for I feel really attached to you for your many sympathies with me, and patience at all my *lunes* . . . Your affectionate friend, John Keats." To Brown he says: "Hunt has behaved very kindly to me"; and again: "The seal-breaking business is overblown. I think no more of it." Hunt's reply is couched in most affectionate terms:

"Giovani [sic] Mio,

"I shall see you this afternoon, and most probably every day. You judge rightly when you think I shall be glad at your putting up awhile where you are, instead of that solitary place. There are humanities in the house; and if wisdom loves to live with children round her knees (the tax-gatherer apart), sick wisdom, I think, should love to live with arms about it's waist. I need not say how you gratify me by the impulse that led you to write a particular sentence in your letter, for you must have seen by this time how much I am attached to yourself.

"I am indicating at as dull a rate as a battered finger-post in wet weather. Not that I am ill: for I am very well altogether. Your affectionate Friend, Leigh Hunt."

This was probably the last letter written by him to Keats. In September Keats went to Rome with Severn to escape the hardships of the winter climate, after having declined an invitation from Shelley to visit him at Pisa. In the same month, Hunt published an affectionate farewell to him in *The Indicator*. An announcement of his death appeared in *The Examiner* of March 25, 1821. The story of the personal relations of the two men could not be better closed than with the words of Hunt written March 8, 1821, to Severn in Rome when he believed Keats still alive:

"If he can bear to hear of us, pray tell him; but he knows it already, and can put it into better language than any man. I hear that he does not like to be told that he may get better; nor is it to be wondered at, considering his firm persuasion that he shall not survive. He can only regard it as a puerile thing, and an insinuation that he shall die. But if his persuasion should happen to be no longer so strong, or if he can now put up with attempts to console him, tell him of what I have said a thousand times, and what I still (upon my honour) think always, that I have seen too many instances of recovery from apparently desperate cases of consumption not to be in hope to the very last. If he still cannot bear to hear this, tell him—tell that great poet and noblehearted man—that we shall all bear his memory in the most precious part of our hearts, and that the world shall bow their heads to it, as our loves do. Or if this, again, will trouble his spirit, tell him that we shall never cease to remember and love him; and that, Christian or infidel, the most sceptical of us has faith enough in the high things that nature puts into our heads, to think all who are of one accord in mind and heart are journeying to one and the same place, and shall unite somewhere or other again, face to face, mutually conscious, mutually delighted."

The literary relations of Keats and Hunt will be considered under two heads; first, the criticism of Keats's writings by Hunt; and second, his direct influence upon them.

On first looking into Chapman's Homer in *The Examiner* of December 1st, 1816, was embodied in an article entitled "Young Poets." It was the first notice of Keats to appear in print and is in part as follows:

"The last of these young aspirants whom we have met with, and who promise to help the new school to revive Nature and

'To put a spirit of youth in everything,'—

is we believe, the youngest of them all, and just of age. His name is John Keats. He has not yet published anything except in a newspaper, but a set of his manuscripts was handed us the other day, and fairly surprised us with the truth of their ambition, and ardent grappling with Nature."

In *Lord Byron and Some of his Contemporaries*, the last line of the same sonnet—

"Silent upon a peak in Darien"—

is called "a basis of gigantic tranquillity."

Leigh Hunt's review of the *Poems* of 1817 was kind and discriminating. He writes characteristically of the first poem, *I stood tiptoe*, that it "consists of a piece of luxury in a rural spot"; of the epistles and sonnets, that they "contain strong evidences of warm and social feelings." This comment is quite characteristic of Hunt. He was as fond of finding "warm and social feelings" in the poetry of others as of putting them into his own. In his anxiety he sometimes found them when they did not exist. He continues: "The best poem is certainly the last and the longest, entitled *Sleep and Poetry*. It originated in sleeping in a room adorned with busts and pictures [Hunt's library], and is a striking specimen of the restlessness of the young poetical appetite, obtaining its food by the very desire of it, and glancing for fit subjects of creation 'from earth to heaven.' Nor do we like it the less for an impatient, and as it may be thought by some irreverend [sic] assault upon the late French school of criticism and monotony." But Hunt did not allow his affection for Keats or his approval of Keats's poetical doctrine to blunt his critical acumen. In summarizing he says: "The very faults of Mr. Keats arise from a passion for beauties, and a young impatience to vindicate them; and as we have mentioned these, we shall refer to them at once. They may be comprised in two;—first, a tendency to notice everything too indiscriminately, and without an eye to natural proportion and effect; and second, a sense of the proper variety of versification without a due consideration of its principles." In conclusion, the beauties "outnumber the faults a hundred fold" and "they are of a nature decidedly opposed to what is false and inharmonious. Their characteristics indeed are a fine ear, a fancy and imagination at will, and an intense feeling of external beauty in its most natural and least inexpressible simplicity."

Hunt was disappointed with *Endymion* and did not hesitate to say so. Keats writes to his brothers:

"Leigh Hunt I showed my 1st book to—he allows it not much merit as a whole; says it is unnatural and made ten objections to it in the mere skimming over. He says the conversation is unnatural and too high-flown for Brother and Sister—says it should be simple, forgetting do ye mind that they are both overshadowed by a supernatural Power, and of force could not speak like Francesca in the *Rimini*. He must first prove that Caliban's poetry is unnatural. This with me completely overturns his objections. The fact is he and Shelley are hurt, and perhaps justly, at my not having showed them the affair officiously (sic); and from several hints I have had they appear much disposed to dissect and anatomize any trip or slip I may have made.—But who's afraid? Aye! Tom! Demme if I am."

Leigh Hunt expressed himself thus in 1828: "*Endymion*, it

must be allowed was not a little calculated to perplex the critics. It was a wilderness of sweets, but it was truly a wilderness; a domain of young, luxuriant, uncompromising poetry."

La Belle Dame sans Merci, which appeared first in *The Indicator*, was accompanied with an introduction by Hunt, who says that it was suggested by Alain Chartier's poem of the same title and "that the union of the imagination and the real is very striking throughout, particularly in the dream. The wild gentleness of the rest of the thoughts and of the music are alike old, and they are alike young." *The Indicator* of August 2 and 9, 1820, contained a review of the volume of 1820. The part dealing with philosophy in poetry is of more than passing interest:

"We wish that for the purpose of his story he had not appeared to give in to the commonplace of supposing that Apollonius's sophistry must always prevail, and that modern experiment has done a deadly thing to poetry by discovering the nature of the rainbow, the air, etc.; that is to say, that the knowledge of natural science and physics, by showing us the nature of things, does away the imaginations that once adorned them. This is a condescension to a learned vulgarism, which so excellent a poet as Mr. Keats ought not to have made. The world will always have fine poetry, so long as it has events, passions, affections, and a philosophy that sees deeper than this philosophy. There will be a poetry of the heart, as long as there are tears and smiles: there will be a poetry of the imagination, as long as the first causes of things remain a mystery. A man who is no poet, may think he is none, as soon as he finds out the first causes of the rainbow; but he need not alarm himself:—he was none before."

Much the same line of discussion is reported of the conversation at Haydon's "immortal dinner," December 28, 1817, when Keats and Lamb denounced Sir Isaac Newton and his demolition of the things of the imagination, Keats saying he "destroyed the poetry of the rainbow by reducing it to a prism." The pictorial features of the *Eve of St. Agnes* were particularly admired by Hunt, as one might be led to expect from the decorative detail of his own narrative poetry. The portrait of "Agnes" (*sic* for Madeline) is said to be "remarkable for its union of extreme richness and good taste" and "affords a striking specimen of the sudden and strong maturity of the author's genius. When he wrote *Endymion* he could not have resisted doing too much. To the description before me, it would be a great injury either to add or to diminish. It falls at once gorgeously and delicately upon us, like the colours of the painted glass." Of the description of the casement window, Hunt asks "Could all the pomp and graces of aristocracy with Titian's and Raphael's aid to boot, go beyond the rich religion of this picture, with its 'twilight saints' and its 'scutcheons blushing with the blood of queens'?" Elsewhere he says that "Persian Kings would have filled a poet's mouth with gold" for such poetry. Hunt calls *Hyperion* "a fragment, a gigantic one, like a ruin in the desert, or the bones of the mastodon. It is truly of a piece with its subject, which is the downfall of the elder gods." Later, in *Imagination and Fancy*, Hunt declared that Keats's greatest poetry is to be found in *Hyperion*. His opinion of the whole is thus summed up:

"Mr. Keats's versification sometimes reminds us of Milton in his blank verse, and sometimes of Chapman both in his blank verse and in his rhyme; but his faculties, essentially speaking, though partaking of the unearthly aspirations and abstract yearnings of both these poets, are altogether his own. They are ambitious, but less directly so. They are more *social*, and in the finer sense of the word, sensual, than either. They are more coloured by the modern philosophy of sympathy and natural justice. *Endymion*, with all its extraordinary powers, partook of the faults of youth, though the best ones; but the reader of *Hyperion* and these other stories would never guess that they were written at twenty. The author's versification is now perfected, the exuberances of his imagination restrained, and a calm power, the surest and loftiest of all power, takes place of the impatient workings of the younger god within him. The character of his genius is that of energy and voluptuousness, each able at will to take leave of the other, and possessing in their union, a high feeling of humanity not common to the best authors who can combine them. Mr. Keats undoubtedly takes his seat with the oldest and best of our living poets."

The more important division of the literary relations of the two men is the direct influence of Hunt's work upon that of Keats.

On Keats's prose style Hunt's influence was very slight and can be quickly dismissed. At one time Keats, affected perhaps by Hunt's example, thought of becoming a theatrical critic. He did actually contribute four articles to *The Champion*. Keats's favorite of Hunt's essays, *A Now*, contains several passages composed by Keats. Mr. Forman considers that "the greater part of the paper is so much in the taste and humor of Keats" that he is justified in including it in his edition of Keats. He has also called attention to a passage in Keats's letter to Haydon of April 10, 1818, which bears a striking likeness to Hunt's occasional essay style: "The Hedges by this time are beginning to leaf—Cats are becoming more vociferous—Young Ladies who wear Watches are always looking at them. Women about forty-five think the Season very backward."

The *Poems* of 1817 show Hunt's influences in spirit, diction and versification. There are epistles and sonnets in the manner of Hunt. *I stood tiptoe upon a little hill* opens the volume with a motto from the *Story of Rimini*. The *Specimen of an Induction* and *Calidore* so nearly approach Hunt's work in manner, that they might easily be mistaken for it. *Sleep and Poetry* attacks French models as Hunt had previously done. The colloquial style of certain passages is significant of Hunt's influence upon the poems. A few examples are:

"To peer about upon variety."

"Or by the bowery clefts, and leafy shelves
Guess where the jaunty streams refresh themselves."

81

"The ripples seem right glad to reach those cresses."

" . . . you just now are stooping
To pick up the keepsake intended for me."

"Of this fair world, and all its gentle livers."

"The evening weather was so bright, and clear,
That men of health were of unusual cheer."

"Linger awhile upon some bending planks
That lean against a streamlet's rushy banks,
And watch intently Nature's gentle doings:
They will be found softer than the ring-dove's cooings."

"The lamps that from the high roof'd wall were pendant
And gave the steel a shining quite transcendent."

"Or on the wavy grass outstretch'd supinely,
Pry 'mong the stars, to strive to think divinely."

The following are infelicitous passages reflecting Leigh Hunt's bad taste, especially in the description of physical appearance, or of situations involving emotion:

" . . . what amorous and fondling nips
They gave each other's cheeks."

" . . . some lady sweet
Who cannot feel for cold her tender feet."

"Rein in the swelling of his ample might."

"Nor will a bee buzz round two swelling peaches."

" . . . What a kiss,
What gentle squeeze he gave each lady's hand!
How tremblingly their delicate ankles spann'd!
Into how sweet a trance his soul was gone,
While whisperings of affection
Made him delay to let their tender feet
Come to the earth; with an incline so sweet
From their low palfreys o'er his neck they bent:
And whether there were tears of languishment,
Or that the evening dew had pearl'd their tresses,
He felt a moisture on his cheek and blesses
With lips that tremble, and with glistening eye,
All the soft luxury
That nestled in his arms."

" . . . Add too, the sweetness
Of thy honey'd voice; the neatness
Of thine ankle, lightly turned:
With those beauties, scarce discern'd
Kept with such sweet privacy,
That they seldom meet the eye
Of the little loves that fly
Round about with eager pry."

Descriptive passages in the Huntian style are not infrequent:
the opening lines from the *Imitation of Spenser* are much nearer
to Hunt than to Spenser.

"Now morning from her orient chamber came,
And her first footsteps touched a verdant hill,
Crowning its lawny crest with amber flame,
Silv'ring the untainted gushes of its rill;
Which, pure from mossy beds, did down distil
And after parting beds of simple flowers,
By many streams a little lake did fill,

Which round its marge reflected woven bowers,
And in its middle space, a sky that never lowers."

These lines of *Calidore* show a like resemblance:

"He bares his forehead to the cool blue sky,
And smiles at the far clearness all around,
Until his heart is well nigh over wound,
And turns for calmness to the pleasant green
Of easy slopes, and shadowy trees that lean
So elegantly o'er the waters' brim
And show their blossoms trim."

A third is:

"Across the lawny fields, and pebbly water."

Single phrases showing the influence of Hunt are: "airy feel,"
"patting the flowing hair," "A Man of elegance," "sweet-lipped
ladies," "grateful the incense," "modest pride," "a sun-beamy tale
of a wreath," "soft humanity," "leafy luxury," "pillowy silkiness,"
"swelling apples," "the very pleasant rout," "forms of elegance."
The following passages apparently bear as close a resemblance
to each other as it is possible to find by the comparison of
individual passages from the works of the two men:

"The sidelong view of swelling leafiness
Which the glad setting sun in gold doth dress"

compare with:

"And every hill, in passing one by one
Gleamed out with twinkles of the golden sun:
For leafy was the road, with tall array."

The *Epistles* are strikingly like Hunt's epistles in spirit, diction and metre. Mr. Colvin has pointed out that the one addressed *To George Felton Mathew* was written in November, 1815, before Keats had met Hunt and before the publication of the latter's epistles; but Keats may have known them at the time in manuscript through Clarke. The resemblances may also have been due, in part, as in other points of comparison, to an innate similarity of thought and feeling.

That Hunt's habit of sonneteering and his preference for the Petrarcan form influenced Keats, is attested by the similarity of the latter's sonnets to Hunt's in form, subjects, and allusions, and by the direct references to Hunt. *On the Grasshopper and the Cricket* and *To the Nile* were written in contest with Hunt. *To Spenser* is a refusal to comply with Hunt's request that he should write a sonnet on Spenser. The title of *On Leigh Hunt's Poem, The Story of Rimini* speaks for itself.

To put it briefly, the *Poems* of 1817 show Hunt's influence in more ways than any equal number of the young poet's later verses. It is seen in Keats's subject matter and allusions; in his adoption of a colloquial style and diction; in his absorption of Hunt's spirit in the treatment of nature and in his attitude toward women; and in his imitation and exaggerated use of the free heroic couplet in *Sleep and Poetry, I stood tiptoe, Specimen of an Induction* and other poems.

Of the poem *Lines on seeing a Lock of Milton's Hair*, written in January, 1818, Keats wrote in a letter to Bailey: "I was at Hunt's the other day, and he surprised me with a real authenticated lock of *Milton's hair*. I know you would like what I wrote thereon, so here it is—as they say of a Sheep in a Nursery Book . . . This I did at Hunt's, at his request—perhaps I should have done something better alone and at home." Leigh Hunt's three sonnets on the same subject, published in *Foliage*, have been already spoken of in the preceding chapter.

Endymion shows a decided decrease in the ascendancy of Hunt's mind over Keats, for the sway of his intellectual supremacy had been shaken before suspicions arose in Keats's mind as to the disinterestedness of his motives. What influence lingers is seen in the general theory of versification and in the diction, with some trace in matters of taste. A marvellous luxury of imagery, glimpses into the heights and depths of nature, an absorbing love of Greek fable, a deeper infusion of the ideal have superseded what Mr. Colvin has called the "sentimental chirp" of Hunt. Specific passages in *Endymion* reminiscent of Hunt are rare, but Book III, ll. 23-30 recalls the general descriptive style in the *Descent of Liberty* and summarizes in a few lines pages of Hunt's diffuse, spectacular imagery. Once or twice Keats seems to have fallen into the colloquial manner in dialogue:

> "But a poor Naiad, I guess not. Farewell!
> I have a ditty for my hollow cell."

Again:

> "I own
> This may sound strangely: but when, dearest girl,
> Thou seest it for my happiness, no pearl
> Will trespass down those cheeks. Companion fair!
> Wilt be content to dwell with her, to share
> This sister's love with me? Like one resign'd
> And bent by circumstance, and thereby blind
> In self-commitment, thus that meek unknown:
> 'Aye, but a buzzing by my ears has flown,
> Of jubilee to Dian:—truth I heard?
> Well then, I see there is no little bird.'"

Occasionally there are passages in the bad taste of Hunt, as this example:

> "Enchantress! tell me by this soft embrace,
> By the most soft completion of thy face,

Those lips, O slippery blisses, twinkling eyes,
And by these tenderest, milky sovereignties—
These tenderest, and by the nectar wine,
The passion—"

Likewise:

"O that I
Were rippling round her dainty fairness now,
Circling about her waist, and striving how
To entice her to a dive! then stealing in
Between her luscious lips and eyelids thin."

In July, 1820, appeared the volume *Lamia, Isabella, The Eve of St. Agnes and other Poems*. The lingering influence of Hunt is seen in a fondness for the short poetic tale, in the direct and simple narrative style, and in the return in *Lamia* to the use of the heroic couplet; but that, along with the other poems of the volume, is free from the Huntian eccentricities of manner and diction found in Keats's earlier works. He had come into his own. In treatment, *Lamia* is almost faultless in technique and in matters of taste; although Mr. Colvin has pointed out as an exception the first fifteen lines of the second book, which he says have Leigh Hunt's "affected ease and fireside triviality." One of the few occurrences of Hunt's manner is seen in the *Eve of St. Agnes*.

"Paining with eloquence her balmy side."

The famous passage in the *Eve of St. Agnes* describing all manner of luscious edibles is very suggestive of one in Hunt's *Bacchus and Ariadne* which enumerates articles of the same kind. It is in this latter poem and in the *Story of Rimini* that Hunt's power of description most nearly approximates to that of Keats. In 1831, in the *Gentle Armour*, Hunt is the imitator of

Keats, as Mr. Colvin has already pointed out.

The peculiarities of Keats's diction are, in the main, two-fold, and may each be traced to a direct influence: first, archaisms in the manner of Spenser and Chatterton; second, colloquialisms and deliberate departures from established usage in the employment and formation of words, in imitation of Leigh Hunt. Keats's theory so far as he had one, is set forth in a passage in one of his letters: "I shall never become attached to a foreign idiom, so as to put it into my writings. The Paradise Lost, though so fine in itself, is a corruption of our language. It should be kept as it is, unique, a curiosity, a beautiful and grand curosity, the most remarkable production of the world; a northern dialect accommodating itself to Greek and Latin inversions and intonations. The purest English, I think—or what ought to be the purest—is Chatterton's."

Keats's *Poems* of 1817 show Hunt's influence in diction more strongly than any of his later works. In the majority of instances, this influence is reflected in the principles of usage rather than in the actual usages, although words and phrases used by Hunt are occasionally found in the writings of Keats. The tendency to a colloquial vocabulary is seen in such words and combinations as jaunty, right glad, balmy pain, leafy luxury, delicious, tasteful, gentle doings, gentle livers, soft floatings, frisky leaps, lawny mantle, patting, busy spirits. Among these words, leafy, balmy, lawny, patting, nest, tiptoe, and variations of "taste" were special favorites with Hunt. A few expressions only of this kind, as "nest," "honey feel," "infant's gums," are found in *Endymion*, and almost none at all in the later poems.

Keats used peculiar words with so much greater felicity and in so much greater profusion than Hunt, exceeding in richness and individuality of vocabulary most of the poets of his own time, that one is forced to believe that Spenser's influence rather than Hunt's was dominant here. Breaches of taste are confined almost entirely to the *Poems* of 1817.

Ordinary words used peculiarly include "nips" (they gave

each other's cheeks), "core" (for heart) and "luxury" (with a wrong connotation), nouns and adjectives employed as verbs, and verbs as nouns and adjectives. These devices likewise cannot be credited to Hunt without reservation, since both Spenser and Milton used them; but there is little doubt that in this instance Hunt was an inciting and sustaining influence. Keats resorted to such artifices frequently and continued to do so to the end. Instances of nouns and adjectives employed as verbs are: pennanc'd, luting, passion'd, neighbour'd, syllabling, companion'd, labrynth, anguish'd, poesied, vineyard'd, woof'd, loaned, medicin'd, zon'd, mesh, pleasure, legion'd, companion, green'd, gordian'd, character'd, finn'd, forest'd, tusk'd, monitor. Verbs employed as nouns and adjectives are: shine, which occurs five times, feel, seeing, hush, pry and amaze.

More examples of coined compounds, nouns and adjectives, are to be found in Keats than in Hunt; in his better work as well as in his early productions. A few are: cirque-couchant, milder-mooned, tress-lifting, flitter-winged, silk-pillowed, death-neighing, break-covert, palsy-twitching, high-sorrowful, sea-foamy, amber-fretted, sweet-lipped, lush-leaved.

The last principle is the coining, or choice of, adjectives in *y* and *ing*; of adverbs in *ly*, when, in many instances, adjectives and adverbs already existed formed on the same stem. The frequent use of words with these weak endings gives a very diffuse effect at times in Keats's early poems. The following are examples: fenny, fledgy, rushy, lawny, liny, nervy, pipy, paly, palmy, towery, sluicy, surgy, scummy, mealy, sparry, heathy, rooty, slumbery, bowery, bloomy, boundly, palmy, surgy, spermy, ripply, spangly, spherey, orby, oozy, skeyey, clayey, and plashy. Adjectives in *ing* are: cheering, hushing, breeding, combing, dumpling, sphering, tenting, toying, baaing, far-spooming, peering (hand), searing (hand), shelving, serpenting. Adverbs are: scantly, elegantly, refreshingly, freshening (lave), hoveringly, greyly, cooingly, silverly, refreshfully, whitely, drowningly, wingedly, sighingly, windingly, bearingly.

These statements are not very conclusive proof of the frequent occurrences of the same words in the poems of the two men. They are questionable even in regard to the principles of usage themselves, since poets of the same period or young poets may possess the same tendencies. Yet in the light of their relations already discussed the similarity of a number of principles seems convincing proof that Hunt influenced Keats considerably in the *principles* of diction in his first volume and occasionally in the selection of individual words; and that Keats never entirely freed himself from some of Hunt's peculiarities. Shelley, in writing of *Hyperion* to Mrs. Hunt, spoke of the "bad sort of style which is becoming fashionable among those who fancy that they are imitating Hunt and Wordsworth." Medwin reported Shelley as saying "We are certainly indebted to the Lakists for a more simple and natural phraseology; but the school that has sprung out of it, have spawned a set of words neither Chaucerian nor Spencerian (*sic*), words such as 'gib,' and 'flush,' 'whiffling,' 'perking up,' 'swirling,' 'lightsome and brightsome' and hundreds of others."

Keats, following the lead of Hunt, used the free heroic couplet in several of the 1817 poems with a license even greater than Hunt's. In *Endymion* he indulged in further vagaries of rhythm and metre that Hunt never dreamed of and in fact greatly disapproved of. Hunt said that "*Endymion* had no versification." In its want of couplet and line units, this is not very far from the truth. Writing of it again in 1828, he says: "The great fault of *Endymion* next to its unpruned luxuriance, (or before it, rather, for it was not a fault on the right side,) was the wilfulness of its rhymes. The author had a just contempt for the monotonous termination of everyday couplets; he broke up his lines in order to distribute the rhyme properly; but going only upon the ground of his contempt, and not having settled with himself any principles of versification, the very exuberance of his ideas led him to make use of the first rhymes that offered; so that, by a new meeting of effects, the extreme was artificial, and much more obtrusive than the one under the old system. Dryden modestly thought, that a rhyme had often helped him to a thought. Mr. Keats in the tyranny of his wealth, forced his rhymes to help him, whether they would or not; and they obeyed him, in the most singular manner, with equal promptitude and ungainliness." *Endymion* has been thought by some critics, to have been written under the metrical influence of Chamberlayne's *Pharronida*. In the number of run-on lines and couplets—a scheme nearer blank verse than the couplet— there is certainly a striking correspondence. Mr. Forman thinks that Keats knew the poem. Mr. Colvin and Mr. De Selincourt can see no real likeness. There is no proof as yet discovered that Keats ever heard of it.

In *Lamia*, after the extreme reaction in *Endymion*, Keats approached nearer to the classic form of the couplet used by Dryden, but still with greater freedom in structure than appears in either Dryden or Hunt. From the evidence of Brown it is probable that Keats imitated Dryden directly and not through the medium of Hunt's work, but it is very likely that Hunt directed him there in the first instance for a model. Mr. Palgrave says of the metre of *Lamia* that Keats "admirably found and sustained the balance between a blank verse treatment of the 'Heroic' and the epigrammatic form carried to such perfection by Pope." Leigh Hunt said that "the lines seem to take pleasure in the progress of their own beauty like sea nymphs luxuriating through the water."

In conclusion, Keats's early and late employment of the couplet was marked always by greater freedom in the use of run-on couplets and lines, and in the handling of the cæsura than Dryden's or Hunt's; he was at first slower than Hunt to employ the triplet and the Alexandrine, but he later adopted them in a larger measure; and he introduced the run-on paragraph and the hemistich independently of Hunt.

KEATS

By Edmund Clarence Stedman

ON the slope of a "peak in Darien," in the shadow of the very ridge where stood the Spaniard,

> . . . when with eagle eyes
> He stared at the Pacific, and all his men
> Looked at each other with a wild surmise,

my fellow-traveller captured a superb blue moth, of a species so rare and so difficult to secure that the natives sell one at the price of a day's labor. We took the beautiful creature with us on our transit, and delicately leashed it that night to the jalousies of our veranda on the plaza of the city of Panama. There, far within the old town, a mate was fluttering around it at sunrise,— to me a miracle, yet one predicted by my friend the naturalist. It is just as safe to predict that young poets will chance upon one another, among millions; "there's a special providence" in their conjunction and forgathering, instinct and circumstance join hands to bring this about. The name of Keats is set within a circlet of other names,—those of Clarke, Reynolds, Hunt, Charles Brown, the artists Haydon and Severn,—each of which is brighter for the fact that its owner gave something of his love and help to the poet whose name outshines them all. The name itself, at first derided as uncouth, has become a portion of the loveliness which once he made more lovely; it belongs to an ideal now so consecrate that all who watched with him, if but for an hour, have some part of our affections. Among these, if last not least, Severn, who shut out his own fair prospects, relieved a comrade's agony and want, accompanied him along the edge of a river that each must cross alone, until, as sings the idyllist, the eddy seized him, and Daphnis went the way of the stream.

Cowden Clarke, Keats's earliest companion in letters, son of his head-master at the Enfield school, first put Spenser into his hands. At the vital moment, when the young poet had begun to plume his wings, Clarke also made him known to Leigh Hunt, of all men in England the one it behooved him to meet. Hunt, whose charming taste was almost genius, had become—and largely through his influence upon associates—the promoter of a renaissance; he went to the Italian treasure-house, where Chaucer and Shakespeare had been before him, and also, like them, disdained not our natural English tongue and the delight of English landscape—the greenest idyl upon earth. In many ways, since fortunate guidance will save even genius years of groping, he shortened the course by which Keats found the one thing needful, the key to his proper song. When the youth settled down for a real effort, he went off by himself, as we know, wrote "Endymion," and outdid his monitor in lush and swooning verse. But it was always Hunt who unerringly praised the finest, the most original phrases of one greater than himself, and took joy in assuring him of his birthright.

Shelley, too, Keats met at this time,—the peer who was to sing his dirge and pæan. Meanwhile, his own heroic instinct, the prescience of a muse "that with no middle flight intends to soar," was shown by his recognition of the greatest masters as he found them,—Chaucer, Spenser, Chapman, Shakespeare, Milton,—and his serious study of few besides. One must have exemplars and preceptors; let these be of the best. Neophytes often are drawn to the imitators of imitators, the catch-penny favorites of the hour, and this to their own belittlement. The blind still lead the blind. Give an aspirant the range of English song, see the masters that attract him, and it is not hard to cast his horoscope.

Pity is akin to love, when not too self-conscious of good

fortune and the wisdom that leads thereto. Keats died so young, and so piteously, that some writers, to whom his work has yielded profit and delight, naïvely regard him from the superior person's critical or moral point of view. Lowell, however, pays honor to the "strong sense" underlying his sensibility. When Mr. Lowell said that "the faults of Keats's poetry are obvious enough," he plainly had in mind the faults of the youth's early work,— extravagances from which he freed himself by covering them in that sculptured monument, "Endymion," with divine garlands and countless things of worth that beguile us once and again to revisit their tomb. Nor can we take him to task for careless rhymes thrown off in his correspondence. Of their kind, what juvenile letters are better, and who would not like to receive the letters of such a poet at play? Keats is the one metrical artist, in his finer productions, quite without fault, wearing by right, not courtesy, the epithet of Andrea del Sarto. Rich and various as are the masterpieces of the language, I make bold to name one of our shorter English lyrics that still seems to me, as it seemed to me ten years ago, the nearest to perfection, the one I would surrender last of all. What should this be save the "Ode to a Nightingale," so faultless in its varied unity and in the cardinal qualities of language, melody, and tone? A strain that has a dying fall; music wedded to ethereal passion, to the yearning that floods all nature, while

> . . . more than ever seems it rich to die,
> To cease upon the midnight with no pain.

Then what pictures, echoes, immortal imagery and phrase! Can a word or passage be changed without an injury, and by whom? The "Ode on a Grecian Urn" is a more objective poem, moulded like the cold Pastoral it celebrates, radiant with the antique light and joy. Could Beauty speak, even thus might she declare herself. We term Keats a Grecian, and assuredly the English lad created, in latest-born and loveliest semblance, the entire breed of "Olympus' faded hierarchy." But what of "The Eve of St. Agnes"? Is it not the purest mediæval structure in our verse—a romance-poem more faultless, in the strict sense of the word, than larger models of earlier or later date? In proportion, color, exquisite detail, it is comparable to some Gothic hall or chapel of the best period; and just as surely "Isabella" is Florentine, and equally without flaw. These poems are none the less charged with high imaginings, Keats being one of the few whose imagination is not lessened by technical supremacy. The sonnet on Chapman's Homer was, in this respect, a foretaste of the large utterance to which he afterward attained. "Hyperion," with its Titanic opening and Doric grandeur of tone inviolate from first to last, was a work which the author, with half his power still in reserve, left unfinished, in the loftiest spirit of self-criticism, avowing that it had too many Miltonic inversions. The word "faults" is, in truth, the last to use concerning Keats. His limitation was one of horizon, not of blemish within its bounds.

As regards verbal expression, a close test of original power, he certainly outranks any poet since Shakespeare. Others are poets and something more, or less,—reformers, men of the world, or, like Körner and Chénier, aglow for heroic action. Keats had but one ambition; he was all poet, and I think he would have remained so. However possible the grotesque changes contrived for Byron and Burns in Hawthorne's fantastic draft of "P's Correspondence," the romancer felt that Keats would never become transformed, and pictured him as still true to the ideal. Shelley worshipped Goodness and Truth in the Beauty to which he vowed that he would dedicate his powers. Of Keats, one may say that his genius was Beauty's other self. In "Wuthering Heights," Catharine Earnshaw avows: "I am Heathcliff! He's always, always in my mind: not as a pleasure, any more than I am always a pleasure to myself, but as my own being." And Keats was Beauty, with the affinity and passion of soul for soul.

It is hard to hold him to account for an early death from inherited tendency to phthisis, aggravated by bleeding at the hands of an old-time surgeon, or for the publication, after sixty years, of his turbid love-letters to Fanny Brawne,—letters in which, though probably the recipient flattered herself otherwise, there is less of the real Keats than in the most trivial verse he ever wrote. If you would know an artist's true self, you must discover it through his art. It was deplorable that these poor letters should be brought to light; let us at least give them no more than their true proportion in our measure of the writer's strength and weakness. Mr. Arnold is warranted in contempt for those who enjoy the one letter that he quotes, and who profess to consider it a "beautiful and characteristic production." It reveals, as he asserts, "complete enervation," and I own that for the moment Keats appears to be "passion's slave." Nevertheless, why yield one jot or tittle to the implication that the old taunt of Blackwood's is sustained by this letter of a "surgeon's apprentice,"—that anything "under-bred and ignoble" can be postulated from even the entire series of these spasmodic epistles? A theory that such a youth as Keats was "ill brought up" cannot be thus deduced; the reverse, all things considered, seems to have been the case. Furthermore, it may be that the evolution of a poet advances quite as surely through experience of the average man's folly and emotion as through a class training in reticence, dignity, and self-restraint. In the first glow of ambition Keats inscribed "Endymion" to the memory of Chatterton, and gladly would have equalled that sleepless soul in fate, so were he equal to him in renown. Afterward, in his first experience of passion, he yielded to morbid sentiment, self-abandonment, the frenzy of a passing hour. It is not out of nature that genius, in these early crises, should be pitifully sensitive or take stage-strides. The training that would forestall this might, like Aylmer's process, too well remove a birth-mark. We can spare, now and then, a gray head on green shoulders, if thereby we gain a poet. Keats was a sturdy, gallant boy at school,—as a man, free from vices patrician or plebeian, and a gentleman in motive and bearing. No unusual precocity of character goes with the artistic temperament. It is observed of born musicians, who in childhood have mastered instrument and counterpoint, and of other phenomenal geniuses, that they are not old beyond their years, nor less simple and frolicsome than their playmates. But the heyday in the blood has always been as critical to poets as the "sinister conjunction" was to the youth of the Arabian tale. Shakespeare, Milton, Burns, Shelley, Byron, were not specifically apostles of common sense in their love-affairs, but their own experience scarcely lowered the tone or weakened the vigor of their poetry. Keats's ideality was disturbed by the passion which came upon him suddenly and late; he clung to its object with fiercer longing and anguish as he felt both her and life itself slipping away from his hold. Everything is extreme in the emotion of a poet. Mr. Arnold does justice to his probity and forbearance, to his trust in the canons of art and rigid self-measurement by an exacting standard; he surely must see, on reflection, that such a man's slavery to passion would be a short-lived episode. Before Keats could rise again to higher things, his doom confronted him. His spirit flew hither and thither, by many paths: across each, as in Tourguéneff's prose-poem, yawned the open grave, and behind him the witch Fate pressed ever more closely. He had prayed "for ten years" in which he might overwhelm himself in poesy. He was granted a scant five, and made transcendent use of them. Had he lived, who can doubt that he would have become mature in character as he was already in the practise of his art? It is to be noted, as regards form, that one of Shelley's most consummate productions was inspired by the works and death of Keats. I doubt not that Keats's sensuous and matchless verse would have taken on, in time, more of the elusive spirituality for which we go to Shelley. As it was, he and Wordsworth were the complements of each other with their respective gifts, and made the way clear for Tennyson and his successors. Impressed by the supreme art and fresh imagination of the author of "Hyperion," not a few are disposed to award him a place on the topmost dais where but two English poets await his coming,—if not entitled there to an equal seat, at least with the right to stand beside the thrones as lineal inheritor, the first-born prince of the blood. His poetry has been studied with delight in this western world for the last half-century. One page of it is worth the whole product of the "æsthetic" dilettants who most recently have undertaken to direct us, as if by privilege of discovery, to the fountain-head of modern song. But

The One remains, the many change and pass.

This prophesying in the name of an acknowledged leader is old as the Christian era. And even the pagan Moschus, from whom, and from Bion, Shelley took the conception of his starry threnody, declares of a dead poet and certain live and unwelcome celebrants:

"Verily thou all silent wilt be covered in earth, while it has pleased the Nymphs that the frog shall always sing. Him, though, I would not envy, for he chants no beauteous strain."

POETRY

ADONAIS

By Percy Bysshe Shelley

I

I weep for Adonais - he is dead!
O, weep for Adonais! though our tears
Thaw not the frost which binds so dear a head!
And thou, sad Hour, selected from all years
To mourn our loss, rouse thy obscure compeers,
And teach them thine own sorrow, say: "With me
Died Adonais; till the Future dares
Forget the Past, his fate and fame shall be
An echo and a light unto eternity!"

II

Where wert thou, mighty Mother, when he lay,
When thy Son lay, pierced by the shaft which flies
In darkness? where was lorn Urania
When Adonais died? With veiled eyes,
Mid listening Echoes, in her Paradise
She sate, while one, with soft enamoured breath,
Rekindled all the fading melodies
With which, like flowers that mock the corse beneath,
He had adorned and hid the coming bulk of death.

III

O, weep for Adonais - he is dead!
Wake, melancholy Mother, wake and weep!
Yet wherefore? Quench within their burning bed
Thy fiery tears, and let thy loud heart keep
Like his, a mute and uncomplaining sleep;
For he is gone, where all things wise and fair
Descend; - oh, dream not that the amorous Deep
Will yet restore him to the vital air;
Death feeds on his mute voice, and laughs at our despair.

IV

Most musical of mourners, weep again!
Lament anew, Urania! - He died,
Who was the Sire of an immortal strain,
Blind, old, and lonely, when his country's pride,
The priest, the slave, and the liberticide
Trampled and mocked with many a loathed rite
Of lust and blood; he went, unterrified,
Into the gulf of death; but his clear Sprite
Yet reigns o'er earth; the third among the sons of light.

V

Most musical of mourners, weep anew!
Not all to that bright station dared to climb;
And happier they their happiness who knew,
Whose tapers yet burn through that night of time
In which suns perished; others more sublime,
Struck by the envious wrath of man or god,
Have sunk, extinct in their refulgent prime;
And some yet live, treading the thorny road
Which leads, through toil and hate, to Fame's serene abode.

VI

But now, thy youngest, dearest one, has perished -
The nursling of thy widowhood, who grew,
Like a pale flower by some sad maiden cherished,
And fed with true-love tears, instead of dew;
Most musical of mourners, weep anew!
Thy extreme hope, the loveliest and the last,
The bloom, whose petals nipped before they blew
Died on the promise of the fruit, is waste;
The broken lily lies - the storm is overpast.

105

VII

To that high Capital, where kingly Death
Keeps his pale court in beauty and decay,
He came; and bought, with price of purest breath,
A grave among the eternal. - Come away!
Haste, while the vault of blue Italian day
Is yet his fitting charnel-roof! while still
He lies, as if in dewy sleep he lay;
Awake him not! surely he takes his fill
Of deep and liquid rest, forgetful of all ill.

VIII

He will awake no more, oh, never more! -
Within the twilight chamber spreads apace
The shadow of white Death, and at the door
Invisible Corruption waits to trace
His extreme way to her dim dwelling-place;
The eternal Hunger sits, but pity and awe
Soothe her pale rage, nor dares she to deface
So fair a prey, till darkness, and the law
Of change, shall o'er his sleep the mortal curtain draw.

IX

O, weep for Adonais! - The quick Dreams,
The passion-winged Ministers of thought,
Who were his flocks, whom near the living streams
Of his young spirit he fed, and whom he taught
The love which was its music, wander not, -
Wander no more, from kindling brain to brain,
But droop there, whence they sprung; and mourn their lot
Round the cold heart, where, after their sweet pain,
They ne'er will gather strength, or find a home again.

X

And one with trembling hands clasps his cold head,
And fans him with her moonlight wings, and cries,
"Our love, our hope, our sorrow, is not dead;
See, on the silken fringe of his faint eyes,
Like dew upon a sleeping flower, there lies
A tear some Dream has loosened from his brain."
Lost Angel of a ruined Paradise!
She knew not 'twas her own; as with no stain
She faded, like a cloud which had outwept its rain.

XI

One from a lucid urn of starry dew
Washed his light limbs as if embalming them;
Another clipped her profuse locks, and threw
The wreath upon him, like an anadem,
Which frozen tears instead of pearls begem;
Another in her wilful grief would break
Her bow and winged reeds, as if to stem
A greater loss with one which was more weak;
And dull the barbed fire against his frozen cheek.

XII

Another Splendour on his mouth alit,
That mouth, whence it was wont to draw the breath
Which gave it strength to pierce the guarded wit,
And pass into the panting heart beneath
With lightning and with music: the damp death
Quenched its caress upon his icy lips;
And, as a dying meteor stains a wreath
Of moonlight vapour, which the cold night clips,
It flushed through his pale limbs, and passed to its eclipse.

XIII

And others came . . . Desires and Adorations,
Winged Persuasions and veiled Destinies,
Splendours, and Glooms, and glimmering Incarnations
Of hopes and fears, and twilight Phantasies;
And Sorrow, with her family of Sighs,
And Pleasure, blind with tears, led by the gleam
Of her own dying smile instead of eyes,
Came in slow pomp; - the moving pomp might seem
Like pageantry of mist on an autumnal stream.

XIV

All he had loved, and moulded into thought,
From shape, and hue, and odour, and sweet sound,
Lamented Adonais. Morning sought
Her eastern watch-tower, and her hair unbound,
Wet with the tears which should adorn the ground,
Dimm'd the aëreal eyes that kindle day;
Afar the melancholy thunder moaned,
Pale Ocean in unquiet slumber lay,
And the wild Winds flew round, sobbing in their dismay.

XV

Lost Echo sits amid the voiceless mountains,
And feeds her grief with his remembered lay,
And will no more reply to winds or fountains,
Or amorous birds perched on the young green spray,
Or herdsman's horn, or bell at closing day;
Since she can mimic not his lips, more dear
Than those for whose disdain she pined away
Into a shadow of all sounds: - a drear
Murmur, between their songs, is all the woodmen hear.

XVI

Grief made the young Spring wild, and she threw down
Her kindling buds, as if she Autumn were,
Or they dead leaves; since her delight is flown,
For whom should she have waked the sullen year?
To Phoebus was not Hyacinth so dear
Nor to himself Narcissus, as to both
Thou, Adonais: wan they stand and sere
Amid the faint companions of their youth,
With dew all turned to tears; odour, to sighing ruth.

XVII

Thy spirit's sister, the lorn nightingale
Mourns not her mate with such melodious pain;
Not so the eagle, who like thee could scale
Heaven, and could nourish in the sun's domain
Her mighty youth with morning, doth complain,
Soaring and screaming round her empty nest,
As Albion wails for thee: the curse of Cain
Light on his head who pierced thy innocent breast,
And scared the angel soul that was its earthly guest!

XVIII

Ah, woe is me! Winter is come and gone,
But grief returns with the revolving year;
The airs and streams renew their joyous tone;
The ants, the bees, the swallows reappear;
Fresh leaves and flowers deck the dead Season's bier;
The amorous birds now pair in every brake,
And build their mossy homes in field and brere;
And the green lizard, and the golden snake,
Like unimprisoned flames, out of their trance awake.

XIX

Through wood and stream and field and hill and Ocean
A quickening life from the Earth's heart has burst
As it has ever done, with change and motion,
From the great morning of the world when first
God dawned on Chaos; in its stream immersed,
The lamps of Heaven flash with a softer light;
All baser things pant with life's sacred thirst;
Diffuse themselves; and spend in love's delight
The beauty and the joy of their renewed might.

XX

The leprous corpse, touched by this spirit tender,
Exhales itself in flowers of gentle breath;
Like incarnations of the stars, when splendour
Is changed to fragrance, they illumine death
And mock the merry worm that wakes beneath;
Nought we know, dies. Shall that alone which knows
Be as a sword consumed before the sheath
By sightless lightning? - the intense atom glows
A moment, then is quenched in a most cold repose.

XXI

Alas! that all we loved of him should be,
But for our grief, as if it had not been,
And grief itself be mortal! Woe is me!
Whence are we, and why are we? of what scene
The actors or spectators? Great and mean
Meet massed in death, who lends what life must borrow.
As long as skies are blue, and fields are green,
Evening must usher night, night urge the morrow,
Month follow month with woe, and year wake year to sorrow.

XXII

He will awake no more, oh, never more!
"Wake thou," cried Misery, "childless Mother, rise
Out of thy sleep, and slake, in thy heart's core,
A wound more fierce than his with tears and sighs."
And all the Dreams that watched Urania's eyes,
And all the Echoes whom their sister's song
Had held in holy silence, cried: "Arise!"
Swift as a Thought by the snake Memory stung,
From her ambrosial rest the fading Splendour sprung.

XXIII

She rose like an autumnal Night, that springs
Out of the East, and follows wild and drear
The golden Day, which, on eternal wings,
Even as a ghost abandoning a bier,
Had left the Earth a corpse. Sorrow and fear
So struck, so roused, so rapt Urania;
So saddened round her like an atmosphere
Of stormy mist; so swept her on her way
Even to the mournful place where Adonais lay.

XXIV

Out of her secret Paradise she sped,
Through camps and cities rough with stone, and steel,
And human hearts, which to her aery tread
Yielding not, wounded the invisible
Palms of her tender feet where'er they fell:
And barbed tongues, and thoughts more sharp than they,
Rent the soft Form they never could repel,
Whose sacred blood, like the young tears of May,
Paved with eternal flowers that undeserving way.

XXV

In the death-chamber for a moment Death,
Shamed by the presence of that living Might,
Blushed to annihilation, and the breath
Revisited those lips, and Life's pale light
Flashed through those limbs, so late her dear delight.
"Leave me not wild and drear and comfortless,
As silent lightning leaves the starless night!
Leave me not!" cried Urania: her distress
Roused Death: Death rose and smiled, and met her vain caress.

XXVI

"'Stay yet awhile! speak to me once again;
Kiss me, so long but as a kiss may live;
And in my heartless breast and burning brain
That word, that kiss, shall all thoughts else survive,
With food of saddest memory kept alive,
Now thou art dead, as if it were a part
Of thee, my Adonais! I would give
All that I am to be as thou now art!
But I am chained to Time, and cannot thence depart!

XXVII

"O gentle child, beautiful as thou wert,
Why didst thou leave the trodden paths of men
Too soon, and with weak hands though mighty heart
Dare the unpastured dragon in his den?
Defenceless as thou wert, oh, where was then
Wisdom the mirrored shield, or scorn the spear?
Or hadst thou waited the full cycle, when
Thy spirit should have filled its crescent sphere,
The monsters of life's waste had fled from thee like deer.

XXVIII

"The herded wolves, bold only to pursue;
The obscene ravens, clamorous o'er the dead;
The vultures to the conqueror's banner true
Who feed where Desolation first has fed,
And whose wings rain contagion; - how they fled,
When, like Apollo, from his golden bow
The Pythian of the age one arrow sped
And smiled! - The spoilers tempt no second blow,
They fawn on the proud feet that spurn them lying low.

XXIX

"The sun comes forth, and many reptiles spawn;
He sets, and each ephemeral insect then
Is gathered into death without a dawn,
And the immortal stars awake again;
So is it in the world of living men:
A godlike mind soars forth, in its delight
Making earth bare and veiling heaven, and when
It sinks, the swarms that dimmed or shared its light
Leave to its kindred lamps the spirit's awful night."

XXX

Thus ceased she: and the mountain shepherds came,
Their garlands sere, their magic mantles rent;
The Pilgrim of Eternity, whose fame
Over his living head like Heaven is bent,
An early but enduring monument,
Came, veiling all the lightnings of his song
In sorrow; from her wilds Ierne sent
The sweetest lyrist of her saddest wrong,
And Love taught Grief to fall like music from his tongue.

XXXI

Midst others of less note, came one frail Form,
A phantom among men; companionless
As the last cloud of an expiring storm
Whose thunder is its knell; he, as I guess,
Had gazed on Nature's naked loveliness,
Actaeon-like, and now he fled astray
With feeble steps o'er the world's wilderness,
And his own thoughts, along that rugged way,
Pursued, like raging hounds, their father and their prey.

XXXII

A pardlike Spirit beautiful and swift -
A Love in desolation masked; - a Power
Girt round with weakness; - it can scarce uplift
The weight of the superincumbent hour;
It is a dying lamp, a falling shower,
A breaking billow; - even whilst we speak
Is it not broken? On the withering flower
The killing sun smiles brightly: on a cheek
The life can burn in blood, even while the heart may break.

XXXIII

His head was bound with pansies overblown,
And faded violets, white, and pied, and blue;
And a light spear topped with a cypress cone,
Round whose rude shaft dark ivy-tresses grew
Yet dripping with the forest's noonday dew,
Vibrated, as the ever-beating heart
Shook the weak hand that grasped it; of that crew
He came the last, neglected and apart;
A herd-abandoned deer struck by the hunter's dart.

XXXIV

All stood aloof, and at his partial moan
Smiled through their tears; well knew that gentle band
Who in another's fate now wept his own,
As in the accents of an unknown land
He sung new sorrow; sad Urania scanned
The Stranger's mien, and murmured: "Who art thou?"
He answered not, but with a sudden hand
Made bare his branded and ensanguined brow,
Which was like Cain's or Christ's - oh! that it should be so!

XXXV

What softer voice is hushed over the dead?
Athwart what brow is that dark mantle thrown?
What form leans sadly o'er the white death-bed,
In mockery of monumental stone,
The heavy heart heaving without a moan?
If it be He, who, gentlest of the wise,
Taught, soothed, loved, honoured the departed one,
Let me not vex, with inharmonious sighs,
The silence of that heart's accepted sacrifice.

XXXVI

Our Adonais has drunk poison - oh!
What deaf and viperous murderer could crown
Life's early cup with such a draught of woe?
The nameless worm would now itself disown:
It felt, yet could escape, the magic tone
Whose prelude held all envy, hate, and wrong,
But what was howling in one breast alone,
Silent with expectation of the song,
Whose master's hand is cold, whose silver lyre unstrung.

XXXVII

Live thou, whose infamy is not thy fame!
Live! fear no heavier chastisement from me,
Thou noteless blot on a remembered name!
But be thyself, and know thyself to be!
And ever at thy season be thou free
To spill the venom when thy fangs o'erflow:
Remorse and Self-contempt shall cling to thee;
Hot Shame shall burn upon thy secret brow,
And like a beaten hound tremble thou shalt - as now.

XXXVIII

Nor let us weep that our delight is fled
Far from these carrion kites that scream below;
He wakes or sleeps with the enduring dead;
Thou canst not soar where he is sitting now -
Dust to the dust! but the pure spirit shall flow
Back to the burning fountain whence it came,
A portion of the Eternal, which must glow
Through time and change, unquenchably the same,
Whilst thy cold embers choke the sordid hearth of shame.

XXXIX

Peace, peace! he is not dead, he doth not sleep -
He hath awakened from the dream of life -
'Tis we, who lost in stormy visions, keep
With phantoms an unprofitable strife,
And in mad trance, strike with our spirit's knife
Invulnerable nothings. - We decay
Like corpses in a charnel; fear and grief
Convulse us and consume us day by day,
And cold hopes swarm like worms within our living clay.

XL

He has outsoared the shadow of our night;
Envy and calumny and hate and pain,
And that unrest which men miscall delight,
Can touch him not and torture not again;
From the contagion of the world's slow stain
He is secure, and now can never mourn
A heart grown cold, a head grown grey in vain;
Nor, when the spirit's self has ceased to burn,
With sparkless ashes load an unlamented urn.

XLI

He lives, he wakes - 'tis Death is dead, not he;
Mourn not for Adonais. - Thou young Dawn,
Turn all thy dew to splendour, for from thee
The spirit thou lamentest is not gone;
Ye caverns and ye forests, cease to moan!
Cease, ye faint flowers and fountains, and thou Air
Which like a mourning veil thy scarf hadst thrown
O'er the abandoned Earth, now leave it bare
Even to the joyous stars which smile on its despair!

XLII

He is made one with Nature: there is heard
His voice in all her music, from the moan
Of thunder, to the song of night's sweet bird;
He is a presence to be felt and known
In darkness and in light, from herb and stone,
Spreading itself where'er that Power may move
Which has withdrawn his being to its own;
Which wields the world with never-wearied love,
Sustains it from beneath, and kindles it above.

XLIII

He is a portion of the loveliness
Which once he made more lovely: he doth bear
His part, while the one Spirit's plastic stress
Sweeps through the dull dense world, compelling there
All new successions to the forms they wear;
Torturing th' unwilling dross that checks its flight
To its own likeness, as each mass may bear;
And bursting in its beauty and its might
From trees and beasts and men into the Heavens' light.

XLIV

The splendours of the firmament of time
May be eclipsed, but are extinguished not;
Like stars to their appointed height they climb,
And death is a low mist which cannot blot
The brightness it may veil. When lofty thought
Lifts a young heart above its mortal lair,
And love and life contend in it, for what
Shall be its earthly doom, the dead live there
And move like winds of light on dark and stormy air.

XLV

The inheritors of unfulfilled renown
Rose from their thrones, built beyond mortal thought,
Far in the Unapparent. Chatterton
Rose pale, - his solemn agony had not
Yet faded from him; Sidney, as he fought
And as he fell and as he lived and loved
Sublimely mild, a Spirit without spot,
Arose; and Lucan, by his death approved:
Oblivion as they rose shrank like a thing reproved.

XLVI

And many more, whose names on Earth are dark,
But whose transmitted effluence cannot die
So long as fire outlives the parent spark,
Rose, robed in dazzling immortality.
"Thou art become as one of us," they cry,
"It was for thee yon kingless sphere has long
Swung blind in unascended majesty,
Silent alone amid an Heaven of Song.
Assume thy winged throne, thou Vesper of our throng!"

XLVII

Who mourns for Adonais? Oh, come forth,
Fond wretch! and know thyself and him aright.
Clasp with thy panting soul the pendulous Earth;
As from a centre, dart thy spirit's light
Beyond all worlds, until its spacious might
Satiate the void circumference: then shrink
Even to a point within our day and night;
And keep thy heart light lest it make thee sink
When hope has kindled hope, and lured thee to the brink.

XLVIII

Or go to Rome, which is the sepulchre,
Oh, not of him, but of our joy: 'tis nought
That ages, empires, and religions there
Lie buried in the ravage they have wrought;
For such as he can lend, - they borrow not
Glory from those who made the world their prey;
And he is gathered to the kings of thought
Who waged contention with their time's decay,
And of the past are all that cannot pass away.

XLIX

Go thou to Rome, - at once the Paradise,
The grave, the city, and the wilderness;
And where its wrecks like shattered mountains rise,
And flowering weeds, and fragrant copses dress
The bones of Desolation's nakedness
Pass, till the spirit of the spot shall lead
Thy footsteps to a slope of green access
Where, like an infant's smile, over the dead
A light of laughing flowers along the grass is spread;

L

And grey walls moulder round, on which dull Time
Feeds, like slow fire upon a hoary brand;
And one keen pyramid with wedge sublime,
Pavilioning the dust of him who planned
This refuge for his memory, doth stand
Like flame transformed to marble; and beneath,
A field is spread, on which a newer band
Have pitched in Heaven's smile their camp of death,
Welcoming him we lose with scarce extinguished breath.

LI

Here pause: these graves are all too young as yet
To have outgrown the sorrow which consigned
Its charge to each; and if the seal is set,
Here, on one fountain of a mourning mind,
Break it not thou! too surely shalt thou find
Thine own well full, if thou returnest home,
Of tears and gall. From the world's bitter wind
Seek shelter in the shadow of the tomb.
What Adonais is, why fear we to become?

LII

The One remains, the many change and pass;
Heaven's light forever shines, Earth's shadows fly;
Life, like a dome of many-coloured glass,
Stains the white radiance of Eternity,
Until Death tramples it to fragments. - Die,
If thou wouldst be with that which thou dost seek!
Follow where all is fled! - Rome's azure sky,
Flowers, ruins, statues, music, words, are weak
The glory they transfuse with fitting truth to speak.

LIII

Why linger, why turn back, why shrink, my Heart?
Thy hopes are gone before: from all things here
They have departed; thou shouldst now depart!
A light is passed from the revolving year,
And man, and woman; and what still is dear
Attracts to crush, repels to make thee wither.
The soft sky smiles, - the low wind whispers near:
'Tis Adonais calls! oh, hasten thither,
No more let Life divide what Death can join together.

LIV

That Light whose smile kindles the Universe,
That Beauty in which all things work and move,
That Benediction which the eclipsing Curse
Of birth can quench not, that sustaining Love
Which through the web of being blindly wove
By man and beast and earth and air and sea,
Burns bright or dim, as each are mirrors of
The fire for which all thirst, now beams on me,
Consuming the last clouds of cold mortality.

LV

The breath whose might I have invoked in song
Descends on me; my spirit's bark is driven
Far from the shore, far from the trembling throng
Whose sails were never to the tempest given;
The massy earth and sphered skies are riven!
I am borne darkly, fearfully, afar;
Whilst, burning through the inmost veil of Heaven,
The soul of Adonais, like a star,
Beacons from the abode where the Eternal are.

KEATS

By Frances A. Fuller

The tall arched windows were flung open wide
To the cool night breeze. Not a shadow hung
Between the world without and he within—
It would have stifled him, his soul so gasped
And struggled for more breath—for room to be!
And with uneven steps treading in haste
Across the floor with moonlight carpeted,
He flung his arms out wildly, as if he
Would part the air pressing too hard around,
As if even space were palpable to him,
And weighed upon his spirit with a might
That crushed his soul like iron. All the while
The big drops of his anguish stood out thick
Upon his pale, broad forehead; and his lips
Were withered with convulsions; and his mouth
Was circled by a rim of ghastly white,
Like that about his eyes, betokening
How well-nigh had the struggle worn him out.
He walked and muttered to himself, and made
All passionate gestures forced by agony,
Till his first strength was spent, then flung him down,
And wept as woman weeps—a flood of tears.
Heaven sent us tears! How would the weak survive
When their great sorrows crush them, if their grief
Were softened by no weeping? Oh, thank God,
Who gives us tears for sorrow's medicine.

And by and by he rose upright, and stood
Once more in the full moonlight, pale and still,
A statue of sweet sorrow: his short curls
Dank and disheveled on his youthful brow;
And his eyes bright with moisture, and the light
Of an unquenchable spirit. Proudly thus,
With a half-conquered anguish at his heart,
He gave his sorrow vocal utterance:

What am I? a poet only,
    A poor poet little gifted;
Yet this creature, low and lonely,
    Once his passionate eyes hath lifted
In a love too fond and daring:
    And for this great sin, O Heaven,
Be his punishment unsparing—
    Be his foul heart stung and riven!

And this poet is ambitious—
    Singing his own songs at pleasure—
Therefore for this wrong malicious,
    The world hates him without measure.
O just world! O tender woman!
    Would my heart like yours were iron!
But because God made it human,
    All these woes its way environ.

Slighted love! and slighted labor!
    Man who in dull hatred passeth
Unjust judgment on his neighbor,
    Sorrow for himself amasseth,
And in turn is scorned and hunted;
    But who breaks by many bruises
The proud heart to kindness wonted,
    Knows his jest the world amuses.

Let me live to brook their smiling—
    God! oh, let me live and strengthen;
I can bear their cold reviling,
    Bear all, if my day thou lengthen.
All, I said—and yet my spirit
    Fainteth at one burning vision—
One wild dream still haunting near it,
    Sweet with love, mad with derision.

O she looked an angel shining
    On me through her golden hair:
Her sweet eyes seemed aye divining
    Some new beauty everywhere:
Smiling out so soft and kindly
    On whate'er she looked upon;
Yet my soul but saw her blindly,
    As if she had been the sun.

O the poet pines for beauty,
    Yet he should not dare approach it!
Far-off worship is his duty:
    E'en the idol would reproach it,
Were his wild devotion nearer;
    Oftener for the brainless rover
Is reserved that other, dearer
    Right to be the loved and lover.

Seeing her thus, why should I love her?
    O it is that fatal sweetness,
Round about her and above her—
    'Tis her beauty's full completeness
That for evermore deceives me,
    Seeming like a soul outshining;
And this falsehood never leaves me,
    But my fond soul still keeps pining.

O God! I am all unworthy,
    Heart and mind are spent and wasted;
And this struggle with the earthy
    Souls of men, my life hath blasted.
But I'll nerve me up to bear it—
    Be a man with men contending;
Hug the mortal while I wear it,
    And hope for a speedy ending.

In Rome are many ruins, and men come
    To weep in pious sorrow o'er an arch
Fallen in fragments—to bewail the doom
    Of broken marble, and to chide the march
Of pitiless time, who yearly covers o'er
    With dust and ivy some affecting show
Of the decay of greatness—to deplore
    A costly edifice's overthrow.

And some, a few, do rouse up the dead past,
    And talk sublimely to the ancient ghosts
Of Cicero and Cæsar, with a vast
    Amount of fancy which deserves their boasts.
The past is a great study—it is well!
    Man should look backward to know where he is:
Then let the pilgrim court the awful spell—
    A pensive, salutary joy is his.

But, O young poet, stay upon your round,
    Your wandering feet beside a brother's tomb,
And gird your spirit up for slight and wound,
    Lest, like the sleeper's, your soul sink in gloom.
A broken heart! ah, 'tis a bitter thing
    To know the gentle in the world must die;
That man must steel his heart by force to wring
    From his unfeeling fellow equity,
Or perish, name and fame, in calumny.

Each blessing has its bane, and thy complaining
    Is that thy gifts are not unmixed with pain;
So finely strung thy heart-chords, some are straining,
    And if they be but touched will snap in twain.
But oh, thy passionate love is not all slighted,
    If from some heart o'erburdened like thine own—
Some fond, weak heart, by pain and passion blighted—
    It wakes on chords long silent their last tone,
And brings back tears and gladness long unknown.

THE POET KEATS

His was the soul, once pent in English clay,
Whereby ungrateful England seemed to hold
The sweet Narcissus, parted from his stream,—
Endymion, not unmindful of his dream,
Like a weak bird the flock has left behind.
Untimely notes the poet sung alone,
Checked by the chilling frosts of words unkind;
And his grieved soul, some thousand years astray,
Paled like the moon in most unwelcome day.

His speech betrayed him ere his heart grew cold;
With morning freshness to the world he told
Of man's first love, and fearless creed of youth,
When Beauty he believed the type of Truth.

In the vexed glories of unquiet Troy,
So might to Helen's jealous ear discourse
The flute, first tuned on Ida's haunted hill,
Against Œnone's coming, to betray
In what sweet solitude her shepherd lay.

Yet, Poet-Priest! the world shall ever thrill
To thy loved theme, its charm undying still!
Hearts in their youth are Greek as Homer's song,
And all Olympus half contents the boy,
Who from the quarries of abounding joy
Brings his white idols without thought of wrong.

With reverent hand he sets each votive stone,
And last, the altar "To the God Unknown."

As in our dreams the face that we love best
Blooms as at first, while we ourselves grow old,—
As the returning Spring in sunlight throws
Through prison-bars, on graves, its ardent gold,—
And as the splendors of a Syrian rose
Lie unreproved upon the saddest breast,—
So mythic story fits a changing world:
Still the bark drifts with sails forever furled.
An unschooled Fancy deemed the work her own,
While mystic meaning through each fable shone.

KEATS

———————————

By Richard Watson Gilder

Touch not with dark regret his perfect fame,
  Sighing, "Had he but lived he had done so";
  Or, "Were his heart not eaten out with woe
  John Keats had won a prouder, mightier name!"
Take him for what he was and did—nor blame
  Blind fate for all he suffered. Thou shouldst know
  Souls such as his escape no mortal blow—
  No agony of joy, or sorrow, or shame!
"Whose name was writ in water!" What large laughter
  Among the immortals when that word was brought!
  Then when his fiery spirit rose flaming after
High toward the topmost heaven of heavens up-caught!
  "All hail! our younger brother!" Shakespeare said,
  And Dante nodded his imperial head.

FOR THE ANNIVERSARY OF JOHN KEATS'S DEATH

By Sara Teasdale

February 23, 1821

AT midnight when the moonlit cypress trees
Have woven round his grave a magic shade,
Still weeping the unfinished hymn he made,
There moves fresh Maia like a morning breeze
Blown over jonquil beds when warm rains cease.
And stooping where her poet's head is laid,
Selene weeps while all the tides are stayed
And swaying seas are darkened into peace.
But they who wake the meadows and the tides
Have hearts too kind to bid him wake from sleep
Who murmurs sometimes when his dreams are deep,
Startling the Quiet Land where he abides,
And charming still, sad-eyed Persephone
With visions of the sunny earth and sea.

KEATS – A SONNET

By Florence Earle Coates

By the pyramid of Caius Sestius,
　　Unmarked for honour or remembrance save
　　By a meek epitaph, there is a grave
For sake of which, o'er oceans perilous,
As to a shrine, uncounted pilgrims come;
　　Each bringing tribute unto one who gave
　　Life beauty,—the one thing man still must crave,
Though worshiping from far, with passion dumb.

The Eternal City by the Tiber holds,
　　In the broad view of Buonarotti's dome,—
　　With all its treasure,—naught that is more dear
Than the low mound that easefully enfolds
　　The English poet who lies buried here
By the pyramid outside the walls of Rome.

BIBLIOGRAPHY

ESSAYS

KEATS BY JAMES RUSSELL LOWELL
First published in *Among My Books*, 1870
ON THE PROMISE OF KEATS
BY GEORGE EDWARD WOODBERRY
First published in *Studies in Letters and Life*, 1890
A READING IN THE LETTERS OF JOHN KEATS
BY LEON H. NINCENT
First published in *The Bibliotaph and Other People,* 1898
KEATS BY BARNETTE MILLER
First published in *Leigh Hunt's Relations with Byron, Shelley and Keats,* 1910
KEATS BY EDMUND CLARENCE STEDMAN
First published in *The Century Magazine, February,* 1884, published again in *Genius and Other Essays*, 1911

POETRY

ADONAIS BY PERCY BYSSHE SHELLEY
First published in 1821, composed in the spring of 1821 after news of Keat's death.
KEATS BY FRANCES A. FULLER
First published in *Poems of Sentiment and Imagination, with Dramatic and Descriptive Pieces,* 1851
THE POET KEATS
First published in *The Atlantic Monthly,* 1858.
Author is not attributed.

KEATS BY RICHARD WATSON GILDER
First published in *The poems of Richard Watson Gilder,* 1908
FOR THE ANNIVERSARY OF JOHN
KEATS'S DEATH BY SARA TEASDALE
First published in *Helen of Troy and Other Poems,* 1911
KEATS – A SONNET
BY FLORENCE EARLE COATES
First published in *The Unconquered Air,*
and Other Poems, 1912

Printed in Great Britain
by Amazon

72013415R00087